KU-300-073

Flesh of My Flesh

Flesh of My Flesh

UNA KROLL

Darton, Longman & Todd
London

First published in Great Britain in 1975 by
Darton, Longman & Todd, Ltd
85 Gloucester Road, London, SW7 4SU

ISBN 0 232 51336 8

Printed in Great Britain by The Anchor Press Ltd
and bound by Wm Brendon & Son Ltd
both of Tiptree, Essex

Contents

For John and Mary,
who have never met except in me

Acknowledgements

Many people have contributed to the preparation of this book. In collecting factual evidence about sexism I have been greatly helped by the staff of the World Council of Churches in Geneva, Miss Pauline Webb, vice-chairman of the W.C.C., and individual delegates to the 'Consultation on Sexism in the 1970s', whom I met in Berlin in 1974, members of the Fawcett Society, 'Women in Media', Women's Rights Campaign, St Joan's International Alliance and the Christian Parity Group.

I would like to thank the publishers, Mr Martin Conway of the British Council of Churches, Mrs Georgie Gatch and Mrs Polly Haslam for reading early typescripts and making valuable criticisms which helped me to prepare the final text. The responsibility for the final text and for any opinions, theories or conclusions expressed therein is mine alone.

I am grateful for the permission to reprint the lines beginning 'I want a revolution like a woman's lover' from a poem called 'Monster', from *Monster: Poems by Robin Morgan* © 1972 by Robin Morgan. Reprinted by permission of Random House Inc.

Then the man said:
  'This at last is bone of my bones
    and flesh of my flesh;
  she shall be called Woman,
    because she was taken out of Man.'
Therefore a man leaves his father and his
mother and cleaves to his wife, and they become
one flesh. And the man and his wife were both
naked, and were not afraid.

(Genesis 2:23–25)

Foreword
by Mary Stott

In the summer of 1974 a group of women working in newspapers, magazines, broadcasting and allied spheres came one evening to an astonishing decision. By a sort of spontaneous combustion an idea flashed into being and then began to take shape. They would try to put up a candidate at the forthcoming General Election who would stand on a women's rights platform.

No one can say, even now, quite how it happened. The women had been working together in close understanding for some time to improve the situation for women, especially by campaigning for an Anti-Discrimination Bill. They had marched together, been through a baptism of fire together at Speaker's Corner, Hyde Park. They had lobbied, sat in the House of Commons gallery during a debate and invisibly hissed, held great meetings, rallied support from all kinds of women's organisations, taken a petition to Buckingham Palace itself.

They had persuaded the press and public to take them and their aims seriously. They were convinced – and many M.P.s agreed – that they had effectively changed the climate of opinion in the country and, most importantly, in Parliament. I believe they felt the compulsion of their joint powers, and that this was what drove them to attempt an impossible task. Both major parties had now promised legislation, but in the state of economic anxiety that was abroad at the time, it seemed all too likely that action would be delayed.

A General Election was practically certain in early October. These women knew the habits of the mass media from the inside. They knew that to launch early in the campaigns a candidate standing specifically for women's rights – the first since Christabel Pankhurst, when women were granted the vote – would draw reporters and interviewers like a magnet and guarantee publicity for their cause. But one thing they did not even have to discuss – the type of women they were seeking. They knew they did not want a Christabel Pankhurst or an Emmeline; nor a Boadicea nor a Joan of Arc, leading hordes of willing but voiceless, voteless, supporters into battle. What they wanted was a *sister*, a woman like themselves but with the degree of courage and commitment which would make her willing to go out in front to be a spokeswoman, a banner-holder, a cynosure for the media's eyes. Anyone who regularly watches TV knows what demands that kind of exposure makes.

So this candidate had to be able to talk in public, think on her feet and keep her cool with needling interviewers. She had to be a woman of exceptional courage and sincerity and to believe deeply and profoundly in women's liberation. And because she would be standing for women's liberation she had, like Caesar's wife, to be above reproach. The hopeful sponsors of the women's rights campaign could hardly believe their good fortune when Una Kroll consented to be their candidate. She had every single one of the qualities they were looking for, but in addition she is a very happy wife and mother, a deaconess of the Church of England, and a family doctor.

When people, women even more often than men, talk with distaste and repulsion of 'women's lib' they do not think of people like Una Kroll. (Nor, incidentally, do they picture the kind of women who sponsored Dr Kroll's candidature, who include several happily married wives, mothers, two grandmothers, and a couple of widows.) Every time anyone says to me, usually after relating with some bitterness an experience of discrimination against women, 'Of course, I'm not Women's Lib', I ask 'What do you mean by Women's Lib?' The answers are seldom specific, but probably the general impression is of fierce young women who are (1) anti-men, (2) anti-family, (3) anti-home life. The whole of Una Kroll's personal and professional life proves that she is none of these things.

That is one of the reasons why her campaign in Sutton and Cheam, though a flop in the electoral sense, was tremendously important as a 'consciousness-raising' exercise. That is one of the reasons why I think her book *Flesh of My Flesh* is important. If a woman like Una Kroll can accept without embarrassment or apology the label 'women's lib' oughn't we, including all good wives and mothers, to ask ourselves whether the equation of Women's Lib with bra-burning and poor Valerie Solanas's 'Society for Cutting up of Men' isn't a media myth?

Myths have astonishing vitality and power of survival, against all reasoned argument or practical experience. It may be that women's liberation is stuck with the disastrous 'bra-burning' myth for ever, and that some new, unsullied label must be found for the movement to set women free to contribute fully to the society in which they live. I have had such rewarding contacts with the movement that I should regret a name change. But the main thing is that the ferment of ideas and self-questioning, by men even more, perhaps, than by women, should continue.

In every day and age there is a majority which clings to the belief that what they are accustomed to is *right* and has the force of natural, or even divine law. But there are also in every generation human beings sensitive to winds of change and new economic and social circumstances who are not afraid to propound new ideas. Of these is Una Kroll. Her book is intensely thought-provoking in an area where emotion has often obscured rational thought. I hope that loving women everywhere will listen to this loving woman.

Introduction

'Experience teaches.'
(Old Latin proverb)

(i)

Twelve years ago we needed a new gas cooker. I went into the nearest showrooms, chose the one that I liked, and said that I wanted to pay for it over an extended period.

'Certainly, madam. We can arrange that for you, but I must ask you to get your husband's signature for the hire-purchase agreement,' said the assistant.

'Why?' I asked. 'I have a good job. I can pay my own debts. Why do you need my husband's signature?'

'It's the rule, madam,' I was told. 'Your husband is the head of the household, so he must sign the agreement, or act as your guarantor.'

I was annoyed, but we needed the gas cooker. I went home and fetched my husband. He was unemployed at the time. He signed the necessary papers, although we both knew that he could neither pay the money himself, nor guarantee to do so in the event of my losing my job.

At the time of this incident, I accepted the assumptions behind the assistant's ruling. Women seldom earned enough to be able to pay considerable debts. They had comparatively poor educational and career opportunities. They received inferior financial rewards for their work, and inadequate pensions on retirement. Women, like myself, learnt to be content with their subordinate position in society because of their important role in the community as the mothers of the next generation of men. Lke many other people, I took it for granted that men had an automatic right to their superior status in society. They needed to take advantage of their better educational opportunities because they would have to support their future wives and children. Men were expected to

fulfil their ambitions and to press on towards higher financial rewards
as they grew older. It was not unusual for them to kill themselves with
overwork before they were able to take advantage of their superior
pensions.

The episode over the gas cooker was no more than a minor irritant,
but soon afterwards I became aware that women suffered considerable
hardship simply because they were women. I also became aware that
men often found themselves imprisoned in sex-determined, stereotyped
roles. I began to learn about the social disease, which is now called
sexism.

Sexism is a coined word which describes 'any attitude, action or
institutional structure which systematically subordinates a person or
group on grounds of sex'. Sexism is a value-loaded word which has
affinities with racism. It does not mean the same as sexual discrimination. This latter term has acquired a pejorative meaning which it does
not deserve, for to discriminate between people on the grounds of sex
is only to identify those features which distinguish them from each
other, without necessarily assigning rank or value to the distinctive
features themselves or to the people who possess them.

When I had learnt more about sexism I became convinced that any
attitude or system which treated people unjustly, simply because of
their sex, was an evil which had to be challenged. I therefore joined
with others to oppose sexism, and to try to free women and men from
its oppression so that they could use their freedom in responsible
partnership with each other for the benefit of the whole community.

Over the past twelve years I have learnt a great deal about the
disease of sexism, and about its victims. I have seen some progress in
the position of women in society, but little improvement in the position
of men or the quality of life which both could hope to enjoy.

Some months ago I was reminded that some fundamental sexist
attitudes and structures have a tenacious hold on people. Our family
again needed a new gas cooker. My husband and I went together to
buy this one. This time the shop assistant was a little more circumspect
than her predecessor. When I inquired about credit facilities she said :
'We normally ask the head of the household to sign the agreement.'
She turned to me. 'Are you the head of your household?'

I sighed. We were faced with the same dilemma as we had been
twelve years earlier. Did the fact that I was the only one able to earn
money outside the home mean that I was the effective head of the
household? Or was my now-retired husband to be reminded once again

that he was responsible for my debts out of his small pension? Did a family need one person at its head?

'What makes someone the head of a household,' I asked. The assistant struggled to find the correct answer.

'Well,' she said, 'usually the man is : unless you're single, divorced or widowed,' she added hastily. Her face showed that she was not too sure that the man by my side really was my husband.

'Never mind,' I said. 'We'll pay for it in cash.' My cheque was accepted without question.*

This more recent episode confirmed my belief that there is still a long way to go before sexism is overcome. Many people remain content with their sexually imposed roles. The majority of people have yet to be convinced that the struggle against sexism is so worthwhile that they wish to be involved in it. This book has grown out of my attempts to understand why sexism has such a tenacious hold on people's lives. I have also tried to envisage what freedom from sexism might mean for the relations between women and men.

(ii)

The plan of this book reflects the history of my encounters with sexism. I first discovered what sexism was by seeing its practical effects on my own life, and on that of other people. I next turned to psychology for help in understanding the roots of sexist attitudes. I thus began a journey which led me to explore what it means to be a human being, and to evaluate the differences between women and men which form the ground of their unity with each other. Some of these facts may be well known : I have reiterated them so as to highlight the absurdity of sexism, which uses these differences between women and men to subordinate the one group to the other.

The middle section of the book is based upon my experiences, and is an account of the journey from the slavery of sexism to the freedom of partnership. I have found that when people become aware of their full potential, and realise that their freedom could help them to make that potential actual, they become involved in conflict and suffering as they take practical steps towards their liberation. This is a painful stage in human development. It is my hope that sharing some of my own experiences on this journey will be of value to other women and men who are travelling in the same direction.

* In England, Scotland and Wales this kind of incident should not occur if the Sex Discrimination Bill becomes law in 1975.

The last two chapters are visionary, because it is only the vision of what liberation might mean to the relations between women and men that sustains many in the present struggle against sexism. The vision has a religious dimension to it, because I believe that the search for wholeness in the human personality and in the relations between women and men unveils a mystery which can only be approached with awe.

(iii)

In writing this book I have been able to draw on my experience as a family doctor. In my work I have seen the results of sexism in many people's lives. I have made use of some real-life case histories, although in every case I have taken care to conceal the identities of the people concerned. I have also made use of the collective experience of a group of people with whom I have worked politically to alter the laws and structures which perpetuate sexism in society. I have been able to widen my perspective by using material which I obtained when I attended the World Council of Churches' 'Consultation on Sexism in the 1970s'. This meeting was held at Johannestift, Spandau, West Berlin, from June 14th to 21st, 1974. As the Consultation was attended by 154 women from 46 different countries this gave me a global picture of the problems which are associated with sexism.

1 Living with sexism in the present-day world

'The pain of sexism is the pain of injustice.'
(Mrs Justice Jiagge, Judge of the Appeal Court in Ghana, 1974)

Sexism, the systematic subordination of people solely on account of their sex, shows itself in many ways. Its effects on people's lives cannot be described in a single portrait. As soon as the picture appears to be complete, another and different aspect of sexism reveals itself and the portrait seems incomplete.

I discovered this when I attended the Berlin 'Consultation on Sexism' in 1974. A group of British women – journalists, broadcasters and television producers – opened the meeting with a presentation of slides and films to illustrate sexist attitudes and practices. After years of experience in this field I did not expect to be surprised at anything I heard or saw. I was quite prepared for the slide we were shown of a woman air pilot, with a journalist's comment below it :

> The first time I see a woman at the controls of a plane I'm travelling on I shall immediately leave the plane, and I expect most of the women passengers to follow me. (Chapman Pincher)

I expected all the material to be as familiar as that, but I was wrong. While a picture of Mother Teresa of Calcutta was being shown, the following quotation was also projected :

> When you come down to it, perhaps women just live too long. Maybe when they get through having babies they have outlived their usefulness – especially now that they outlive men by so many years ! (Edmund Overstreet, gynaecologist)[1]

This juxtaposition of words and picture made a strong impression on me, for I had not realised that, in the twentieth century, any intelli-

B

gent person could tie a woman so closely to her biological function as to think of her as a disposable object. I had seen an aspect of the subject that I had not seen before.

Sexism often allies itself with other factors which oppress the lives of ordinary people. It would be naive to think that it is the only factor or even the greatest factor, in the unhappiness which faces many people in the various societies which make up our present-day world. In this chapter I am going to illustrate what it is like to live with sexism by describing the lives of some of the people whom I have met in person, and by recounting facts which I knew to be accurate at the end of 1974. In the following descriptions the people and incidents portrayed are real ones, although I have concealed the identities of the people concerned.

Sexism in people's lives

Julie was unhappy. She had left school when she was fifteen and had worked as a shop assistant for two years before she had married. The birth of three children at yearly intervals had exhausted her. She was also undernourished and anaemic.

Julie's housekeeping allowance was quite inadequate for the needs of the family. She did not know how much her husband, Ron, earned. Whenever she asked him for an increase in her weekly spending money, to offset the rise in the cost of living and the increased needs of their growing children, she was greeted with abuse and stubborn refusal.

Ron spent little time at home. Julie suspected him of adultery. When she found out that she was right, she became depressed and came for medical help. She admitted that she would like to leave her husband if she could, but she had nowhere to go. The rent book for their council house was in Ron's name. Julie had not been able to save any money and had no skilled occupation by which to support herself and the children. If she left the marital home she would be guilty of desertion, and since she would not be technically homeless, could not expect to be rehoused by the council. She was trapped by circumstances.

Julie had been brought up to think that marriage was the happiest fulfilment of a woman's life. After only five years of married life Julie was faced with lifelong misery. There was no escape from it : drugs might alleviate her depression; they could not cure her situation.

Another woman, Maria, had had four children. Her husband, Bill, was sick with a pathological jealousy. He constantly accused Maria of infidelity. He followed her whenever she went out in the evening. At odd intervals during the day he rang up from work to make sure that she was in the house. He even refused to allow her to see a male doctor.

Maria found a woman doctor. She explained her plight and asked to be sterilised. She felt that she could not face the burden of more children when she had such a sick husband.

Unfortunately, at that time Bill's written consent was mandatory before such an operation could be performed. Despite every persuasion Bill refused his permission for the operation. He thought it would give Maria the chance of living promiscuously. For medical reasons Maria could not take oral contraceptives. After she had had two more children, her husband became so ill that he attacked her with a carving knife and had to be forcibly removed to mental hospital.

Maria was left alone with six children. They lived on social security below the poverty line. Bill remained in hospital.

Theresa was a widow, with a five-year-old child. She lived on social security because she found it hard to find work which would fit in with her child's school hours and pay her enough wages to support them both.

Theresa was only twenty-five years old when she was widowed. One day she was accused of cohabiting. A neighbour had seen a man leaving her house early one morning, and, out of spite, had reported the fact to the social security offices. Special investigators visited Theresa, accused her of drawing social security under false pretences, and summarily removed her pension book, solely on the suspicion that she was being supported financially by her lover.

Without her social security book Theresa found herself without means of support. She admitted that she had sexual intercourse with her friend, but said that he neither supported her, nor intended to marry her. Their mutual loneliness had drawn them together, but they had recognised that they were not really suited to each other. Now Theresa found herself alone, humiliated and afraid.

Theresa won her case on appeal to a special tribunal after five months of anxious waiting. She had been deeply hurt by the experience. She had become afraid to make any further relationship with a man and so denied herself any chance of making another and more fruitful relationship.

Julie, Maria and Theresa were penalised because of certain attitudes and presumptions of a sexist society. Julie had assumed that marriage would automatically guarantee her financial stability for life. Maria came up against the assumption that a woman had no rights over her own body. Theresa was victimised by society's presumption that any woman who had had sexual intercourse with a man was supported by him.

The effects of sexism are most obvious in women. Men can find themselves equally victimised by social expectations and role stereotyping.

James, a pleasant young man, was a junior executive in a large industrial firm. His father, on the other hand, had never risen above the position of chief cashier in a bank. James's mother had despised her husband for his seeming failure so she had determined that her son should succeed in everything he did. She had sacrificed her own interests to his needs. She had seen that he had special coaching at school. When James succeeded in his school and university examinations, her pride in him knew no bounds. She was pleased when James married a rich young woman, Vanessa. Between them, the two women set out to make James into the perfect top executive.

After ten years of hard work under these pressures, James began to suffer from disabling attacks of palpitations of the heart and anxiety. He was caught in a circumstantial web from which only illness could save him. By this time, he could no longer admit to himself that he was not the sort of person his mother and wife wanted him to be. He had neither the ambition nor the ruthless drive to pursue the career they had mapped out for him. James became the victim of a cardiac neurosis. A 'bad heart' was the only respectable way by which he could retire from the firm without losing his self-respect. In early middle age James became a cardiac invalid. A year later, Vanessa left him for a more successful man.

William, by contrast was a very successful man. He had been brought up by an overpowering, brilliant mother. During that process he had acquired a defensive dislike of all clever women.

William became a university professor. He was an excellent teacher who always took good care to keep his women students in their place. His sarcastic wit at their expense was highly amusing. He became widely known as a misogynist and eccentric wit. He found himself increasingly isolated in a role which he despised, but from which he could not escape.

Sometimes William found himself longing for the company of a woman. All his attempts at making a permanent relationship failed because, just as the relationship was deepening, his cruel wit would take over and destroy it. His self-hatred turned to deep depression. He could no longer live with the side of himself he despised. His pride prevented him from seeking medical help.

No one really understood why, at the height of his career, William killed himself.

Phillip's case was different. He was a gentle, home-loving man who was a good amateur artist. He was married to Jean, a school teacher who enjoyed her career. Phillip had a job as an office clerk, but he hated it.

When their first baby was on the way, Phillip and Jean made a mutual decision that as soon as their baby was old enough, Phillip would give up his job and look after the child, while his wife returned to her work. Jean could easily earn enough to support the three of them. Phillip would be able to enjoy the homemaking he loved, and he hoped to develop his artistic talent as well.

Both of them were unprepared for the outraged reactions of their relatives, the neighbours and even the milkman and postman, who found such behaviour incomprehensible. The young parents did not let these psychological pressures spoil their happiness, nor did they alter their chosen way of life. In time, people began to get used to it.

Two years later, Jean fell ill with pneumonia. It was then that she discovered that so far as sickness benefit and social security were concerned she was treated as if she were a single woman. Indeed, her cash benefit was less than than she would have drawn as a single woman. Jean was very ill for some time and nearly died. She realised that if this had happened her husband and child could have been left without a widower's pension.

Phillip returned to work. Jean struggled slowly back to health. Their relatives congratulated them on their return to normality. Phillip and Jean resigned themselves to a conventional way of life for the sake of their family's security.

James, William and Phillip were the victims of sexist attitudes and structures as much as the women. James tried to conform to what was expected of him. William was trapped by his upbringing. Phillip tried to alter his life style and might have succeeded but for the social barriers placed in his way.

The people whom I have described did not develop their sexist attitudes overnight. These attitudes have a long gestation period. They are the result of social and cultural conditioning which begin in the home and continue at school.

Sexism in education

Education begins in the family. It takes place through the conscious efforts of parents, and also through their unconscious influence on their children. I can illustrate how these influences affect girls and boys by telling the stories of two children who were born in the same year as each other, on the same housing estate of a city suburb. The fathers of both children were skilled artisans.

Barbara was a first child whose parents were near middle age when she was born. Her arrival was a joyful occasion. Barbara's father had wanted a daughter, because he thought that an older woman would find a girl easier than a boy to bring up.

Barbara grew up in a happy and secure home. Her mother did not go out to work. She enjoyed motherhood, and took a special delight in making all her daughter's pretty clothes.

Barbara was a clever child. She went to a girls' grammar school. At one time she wanted to be a doctor, but when she went to see her careers mistress about it she was firmly discouraged. She was told that it was harder for a girl to get into medical school than it was for a boy. She was warned of the difficulties she would find if she tried to combine a medical career with marriage. In the end, Barbara chose to become a nurse. Her mother was glad. She had never said so aloud, but her own hope was that Barbara would soon get married and settle down to the proper work of a woman, as a wife and mother.

By the time that Barbara was eighteen, she expected that work would take a secondary place to homemaking, so far as her own life was concerned. She was confident of herself as an attractive young woman, but she had a low opinion of her ability to undertake competitive work outside the home.

Tony was also a first child. When he was born his father was exultant. He felt that he had reproduced himself and safeguarded the family name. He promised himself that he would start his own business, so that when the boy grew up he could inherit it as a going concern.

Tony's mother was delighted, too. She had wanted a son, and as there were no other boys in her own family, she knew that her parents would rejoice. She clothed her baby son in blue, and the whole family celebrated his arrival with a grand christening party.

By the time that he was two years old, Tony was car mad. He discarded his teddy bear in favour of a fork-lift truck which he took to bed each night.

In the first four years of his life, Tony split his head open and had to have stitches inserted. He spilt a kettle of boiling water over his legs. He climbed better than most boys of his age, and was always up to mischief. He fought boys who were older than himself. He had already upset the neighbours badly when he had poked a stick into their daughter's eye.

His father refused to allow his son to be punished. He was proud of his son's physical strength. As Tony grew up he was encouraged to be out-going, adventurous and ambitious. He learnt to understand machinery, and knew how to repair the family car.

By the time he left school, after A-levels, Tony was confident about his own future. He expected to go to college before joining his father in the family business. He had passed his driving test. He had a girl friend. He looked forward to marriage. He was ready for life.

In growing up, Barbara and Tony had discovered what sort of behaviour was expected of women and men. Their families' expectations for them had been reinforced by their formal education. They had been exposed to massive social conditioning through advertising and the media. Unacceptable personality traits had been dealt with by suppression or repression. Barbara had suppressed her ambition for a career. Tony had repressed his gentleness. Later, they would probably dislike other people who exhibited those traits which were inadmissible to themselves. Barbara might, for instance, be disparaging about women who pursued careers, especially if they had children as well. She would probably choose a male doctor for her own family, and might dislike all women in authority. Tony might well become contemptuous about gentle men, dismissing them with the thought that they were bound to be homosexuals.

Childhood conditioning leaves its marks on the development of personality. Psychological conditioning is often strongly reinforced by the formal educational system.

In Western society children learn to read from picture books. In Great Britain nearly all the early reading material is sexist. In saying that, I mean that mothers and fathers are portrayed as people who have very different and unequal roles in life. The mother is nearly always shown at work inside her own home, cleaning, cooking, washing and caring for the children. If she is seen at work outside the home, she will usually be cast in a supporting role to a man, for instance, as a nurse or secretary. The father is depicted as an important person, often having exciting jobs like those of a surgeon, an air pilot or an engine driver.

Children in books are portrayed in much the same way. A girl is pictured helping her mother to do the washing up, or is shown playing with dolls. Boys are seen to be people who do adventurous things like climbing trees, flying kites or scaling rocks.

A great deal of role conditioning takes place through the influence of advertisements which children absorb even before they can read.

Primary-school education reinforces what the children have already absorbed in their pre-school years. Girls and boys receive the same kind of education but not the same opportunities. For instance, in some areas in Britain, where children pass from their primary school to their secondary school at the age of eleven, through a selective examination system, girls are marked down in the examination so that fewer of them are able to get into an academic-type grammar school. This is done because at this age, by the normal process, far more girls than boys would qualify for academic schooling.

Of the girls in Britain leaving school before the age of eighteen, only 7% go into apprenticeships as compared with 38% of boys. Less than a quarter of girls leaving school take any job training. 36% of boys under the age of eighteen are able to pursue further training through the day release scheme, whereas only 9.2% of girls are given the same opportunity.

Only 8% of young women go on to higher education compared with 22% of men. Sex quotas still exist in some fields of university education, as in veterinary-science colleges, law schools and some medical colleges. However, recently some medical schools have admitted a far higher proportion of women than formerly. Figures for 1974 show that, overall, women now constitute 31% of medical-school applicants and 33% of the intake.[2]

I have quoted these facts which were accurate at the beginning of 1974, from the statistics for one European country, to show the kind of factors which operate against women in the field of education.* In many instances the over-emphasis on the education of boys places undue pressure on less able boys, so that those who cannot measure up to the high standards expected of them feel that they are failures.

In some countries girls and boys get better educational opportunities than in Britain. For instance, in the U.S.S.R. 48% of students receiving higher education are women. In East Germany the picture has altered dramatically since 1949 when only 18.6% of university students

* The Sex Discrimination Bill (1975) gives women and men equal educational opportunities in law.

were women. By 1972 women formed 40.8% of the student population. In Cuba there were 56% of girls receiving secondary education, and 43% of university students were women.

Nevertheless, in Great Britain women do much better than in many other countries. Throughout the world there are 468 million people who are illiterate. In 1974, 60% of these were women. In Brazil, 43% of women cannot read. In Latin America educational opportunities for girls hardly exist. In the Dominican Republic, for instance, girls make up only 1.1% of the school pupils. In India, despite the fact that the Prime Minister is a woman, millions of women are illiterate, and live under conditions of domestic and feudal exploitation.[3]

I have been able to give only a brief summary of the differences which exist between the educational systems of various cultures which I have studied over a period of time. I believe that these differences are important because they partly account for the contrasting attitudes of Western, Second-World and Third-World women to the problem of sexism.

At the 'Consultation on Sexism' in Berlin, representatives of these different sections of the world came together. It was noticeable that women approached the problems associated with sexism along lines which indicated which part of the world they came from. For instance, many Western women suffered from internalised inferiority feelings. They had been the victims of sexist attitudes and structures in societies where the men were relatively affluent. The Second-World women were far more confident than the Western feminists. They felt that some of the problems facing women had been overcome already in their countries, through policies which made equality of educational opportunity mandatory for women and men. The Third-World women had difficulty in understanding the feminist attitudes of the Western women. They were much more concerned about human liberation from universal evils like hunger, poverty and political oppression than about feminist aspirations. They tended to look towards the Second-World political policies to solve the problems of the underprivileged peoples of the countries from which they themselves came. It was obvious to everyone at the Consultation that Western and Second-World women had more advantages than the men of the Third World. We were all agreed that the Third-World problems should receive priority. At the same time, evidence from the Second World showed that even in those countries women faced greater difficulties in the field of employment than men.

Sexism in employment

In a European country like Britain, women and men have very different expectations with regard to work outside the home.

The labour force in Britain numbers 22 million people. Of these, 9 million are women. The country could not get on without its female workers, but 90% of the women in this labour force work at unskilled jobs. They are in work designated as 'women's work'. These women cannot hope to profit from the 1971 Equal Pay Act, when it comes into force at the end of 1975. In the interim period, many firms are changing their pay structures so as to avoid having to pay women and men equally. Other firms will continue to operate a sex differential through fringe benefits which will not be covered by the Equal Pay Act.

In April 1973 the average weekly earnings before tax were :

> Male manual workers : £37.00
> Female manual workers : £19.00
>
> Male non-manual workers : £47.80
> Female non-manual workers : £24.00

These figures might be acceptable if women were only going out to work to earn money which would pay for extra luxuries in their families, but the evidence shows otherwise. Of the 9 million working women in Britain 44% are single, separated, divorced or widowed. A high proportion of these women are dependent on the money they can earn through their own labour.

These figures mean that in those families where the woman is the main wage earner, the average income will be only just over half that of a family where the man is the chief support. As 90% of women still earn less than £25.00 a week, this is a serious handicap to a single-parent family, to single women who have elderly relatives to care for, and to married women whose husbands are unable to work.[4]

Apart from the economic handicaps facing women in employment, their opportunities for promotion are fewer than those of men. This is partly because many woman retire temporarily from work to have their children, at a time when men of comparable age are rapidly acquiring valuable experience at work. However, this cannot be the only reason, because single women also find promotion difficult to come by. The House of Lords Select Committee heard overwhelming evidence of this in the facts presented to them in 1972–73. One instance of the poor prospects of women is in the teaching profession, where the majority of teachers in the country are women, but where the majority of headships go to men. For example, in January 1971, there were 994 mixed comprehensive schools in Britain of which only 53 had women teachers as headmistresses.[5]

It is interesting to note that in 1873 a girl of seventeen years, signing only her initials A.M.A.H.R., sat for the senior Oxford examination. On the assumption that she was a male she was granted an exhibition to Worcester College. When it was discovered that she was a woman she was presented with a collection of books in place of the scholarship she had won.[6] In 1973 a woman applied to a national newspaper for a senior post. She did not indicate her sex on the application form, but listed her excellent qualifications and experience for the job. She received a warmly worded invitation to go for an interview. When she went to it, she was greeted with undisguised surprise, and was told that women were not employed at such a senior grade in that newspaper.[7]*

Britain is matched by most European countries with regard to employment. In Holland about 25% of married women work outside their homes. There is no law on equal pay yet, although one has been promised for 1975. In Belgium 60 out of every 100 married women work, but there is little training for them, and they are directed to unskilled jobs. In France there is a serious lack of vocational training for women, and there is an average difference of 33% between women's wages and men's, the men being the higher paid. In Italy an Equal Pay Act was passed in 1948. but women's jobs are always placed in the lowest-paid category. In 1974 an Act was passed forbidding the dismissal of women on marriage. This had been a widespread practice. Employers can still get round this act and do. They simply demand impossible hours of work from their married women, and the women give up through exhaustion.[8]

In many non-European countries the conditions of work for women are very poor. For instance, in Japan there are college graduates who are required to clean the room in which they and their male colleagues work, and they must arrive thirty minutes before the men in order to do this extra task. They are expected to serve the men with tea at any time of the day. In many industries, women are forced to retire at the age of thirty. In Sri Lanka women domestic servants work from 6.00 a.m. to 10.00 p.m. and there is no legislation to protect them from exploitation. Black women in South Africa are at the bottom of the

* Theoretically this should not happen if the Sex Discrimination Bill (1975) becomes law.

ladder. Of all working women more than half work in domestic service. Another quarter are farm labourers. The women who do manage to get a good education suffer from a double disability of sex and colour of skin. A black 'nursing sister' can earn only half the money that a white 'nursing sister' can. In Asia there is no deliberate policy which penalises women on account of their sex, but the overall poverty of member countries means that labour is exploited wherever possible. Women are an especially vulnerable section of the community and they suffer accordingly. Where the feminist protest is very articulate, as in the United States of America and Canada, women do better, particularly when they form or join strong unions, but even in these countries the fight to secure decent working conditions and equal employment rights is an uphill one.[9]

In Second-World countries legislation is very favourable to women, but they still find that they do some of the heaviest manual labour while the men become their overseers. Women are still expected to sacrifice themselves. An East German woman, Christa Lewek, gave a vivid example of this in a paper which she presented in West Berlin. First she quoted the law which governs relations between wife and husband in her country :

Section 66. Para:10.1

Both spouses must play their part in bringing up and caring for the children and in running the home. The relationships between the spouses must be so regulated that the wife is able to combine her professional and social activities with motherhood.

She went on to describe a not uncommon situation in which two people had both worked at skilled occupations until their two sons had been born :

There was no grandmother around and the problems began. Somebody had to leave work on time, fetch the children from the nursery, do the shopping . . . There were angry arguments about this between my husband and myself, because there was always something happening in his foreman's section which kept him on for another hour or two. But I was also needed; my brigade was working on a complicated plan, which had only just started. In the end it all became too much for me and, at my request, I gave up my brigadier work, but with the assurance from my husband ringing in my ears that when he had finished his foreman's course it would be my turn . . . but someone has to look after the children! The house has to be cared for. And it is always the woman who suffers. There have been plenty of arguments about that, between my husband and me.

In a survey for the East German women's magazine *Für Dich*, it was found that 78.8% of the housework is still done by women, while men do 13% and children 8.2%.[10]

This story illustrates a universal dilemma. Women are the only workers who actually produce the next generation work force. This work of child bearing and rearing is valuable to the whole community. Yet it is rewarded (by society as a whole) as if it were not work at all, even though all societies pay lip service to the importance of motherhood.

Sexism in family life

In Britain most women give up work when their first child is born. Many rightly feel that the work of motherhood is very important during their children's early years of life. They wish to stay at home until their youngest child goes to school. A smaller number of women give up work outside the home when they marry and never return to paid work again, although they continue to serve the community in which they live in many different ways.

The free choice of one's life style is important in any society. There are many families where the work that women do within their homes is highly valued by their husbands and children, and where the women feel completely fulfilled. Sexism does not enter family life at all unless individual women are subordinated by attitudes which devalue them as human beings. Family life is centred on relationship. It is an area of living where firm facts about sexism are hard to obtain, and even harder to evaluate.

For instance, many women's liberation groups throughout the world demand that women should have the right to know what their husbands earn. Their husbands do have the right to know what they earn. In 1974 a Canadian lawyer and sociologist, Dr Kieth Feandel, a former labour relations adviser to the Canadian Prime Minister, carried out a comparative study in a number of countries. He reported on the percentage of women who did not know what their husbands

earned. In Britain seven husbands out of ten did not tell their wives
how much they earned. In France five in ten men concealed their pay
slips. In West Germany only four in ten succeeded in keeping the secret.
In the United States of America the situation was totally different.
There, less than one in a hundred men maintained silence on the size
of their earnings. Nevertheless, although British husbands led the world
in concealing their earnings from their wives, they actually handed over
more money to their wives than anywhere else in the world. It would
be unwise to make any deductions about the attitudes of men towards
their wives from these figures !

Although sexist attitudes within the family may not easily be proven,
structures in society are more open to evaluation. In Britain the work of
a full-time housewife has been valued at £2000 a year to her
family. If assessed as part of the Gross National Product, women's
work in the home would account for 39% of the total figure. If a
housewife falls ill for more than a few days the family begins to recognise her worth. The so-called 'housekeeping allowance', sometimes
called 'the wife's wages', does not begin to cover the economic cost of
her work. Widowers find this out when they have to hire paid help to
look after their homes. In their case the State allows them income tax
relief if they have to employ a housekeeper, but no such income tax relief
is available for widows. It is automatically assumed that a widow can
manage the housework as well as having to go out to work to earn
money to support herself and her family.

In economic terms the domestic role of women is undervalued in
Britain. In 1974, for instance, a single woman who gave up work to care
for infirm elderly relatives not only forfeited her earnings but also
jeopardised any form of retirement pension or other social insurance
benefit. A married woman was not fully covered by social security. If
she worked at paid employment and paid the full insurance contributions she was allowed to, her benefits would still be lower than those
received by a single woman. If she did not work outside the home she
had no way of paying contributions so that she could draw financial
help in the event of her illness or disablement.*

In 1974, Britain did not give motherhood priority. Britain continued to be at the bottom of the European Economic Community in
the statutory provision of maternity leave. Whatever her circumstances, whenever a woman left a firm to have a child, she had no automatic right to be re-employed by that firm. In other countries, such as
West Germany, Italy and France women knew that their jobs were

* Tax, social security benefits and pensions are not covered by the Sex Discrimination Bill (1975).

secure for a definite period while they took maternity leave. Maternity grants and benefits were also lower in Britain than in all other European countries except Ireland. There was no provision for guaranteed maintenance allowances to single-parent families, which would have enabled the unsupported mother or father to choose to stay at home or to go out to work. There was no family allowance for the first child. Family allowances for the other children had remained unchanged in amount for six years, despite inflation. Any society which undervalues motherhood in this way has not acknowledged the worth of women to the health and welfare of the whole community.[11]*

In 1973, it was estimated that there was a shortfall of 80,000 places for the children of 'priority' groups who needed crèche or day nursery facilities. Registered child-minders received no official training, and this skilled work was normally rewarded by inadequate payment, some child-minders receiving sixty to eighty pence for a whole day's care of another person's child.[12]

In 1974, a woman was still her husband's legal inferior. Her earnings were considered to be part of her husband's income for tax purposes, unless the couple specifically requested otherwise. If a wife had no income of her own she had no legal right to any part of her husband's income, other than half of what she could save out of her housekeeping allowance. About 90% of marital homes were still owned by the husband, and unless a wife registered her right to occupancy, her husband could sell the house without her consent. If an elderly couple decided on legal separation the husband would receive £10.00 of the weekly State pension and his wife only £6.00. This kind of legalised inequality in the distribution of the State pension reflects the fact that a man's work outside the home during his active working life is considered to be more important than his wife's equally hard work inside the home. Her contribution to the family income is a hidden and therefore unrecognised asset.

In Britain, women were also penalised for their longevity. In the graduated State pension scheme women had to pay £9.00 for every 2½-pence unit of pension benefit, while men paid only £7.50 for each unit. This is a considerable financial penalty for the misfortune of living longer on average than most men.[13]

In 1974 many married women were unable to enter into mortgage arrangements, or to make hire-purchase agreements, without their husbands' written consent and guarantee. This applied even when the women were the breadwinners in the family (but see p. 15).

* Limited legislation is under way to help working mothers and single parent families.

At present, the evidence shows that in Britain, women are regarded as assets within their families, but they are assets which continue to be undervalued, not least by women themselves. This low opinion of the worth of women is shown also in the paucity of women in the public and political life of most countries in the world.

Sexism in politics and public life

In October 1974, 29 women were elected to the British House of Commons. They made up 4.2% of the total membership. In Holland, 14% of members of Parliament were women, but only one was a minister of state. In Denmark, women obtained 15% of the seats in parliament. These figures compare unfavourably with countries like the U.S.S.R., where women comprise 30% of members of the Praesidium and 45% of delegates to local Soviets. In Britain, the proportion of women standing for election to Parliament has gradually risen. In 1970, there were 99 candidates; in February 1974, 143, and in October 1974, 156: yet for the last fifteen years the proportion of women actually elected to Parliament has scarcely altered.[14]

In Local Authority government the figures are equally discouraging. The Maud report of 1967 found that only 12% of councillors were women, who were mostly over sixty-five years of age. Only 10% of committees were chaired by women.

In 1974 women were under-represented on every Public Body and were altogether absent from some. Out of twenty-eight Public Boards only seven had any women members. On industrial tribunals women members make up only 11% of a total membership of approximately 1350.[15]

There were very few women shop stewards, Trades Union officials or national executive officers. For instance, the National Union of Teachers of whose members 74% are women, had only seven women on their Executive body of forty-three members, and only two women among its thirteen officials.[16]

In terms of sexism, the Church of England, which is established by law, does not differ greatly from secular institutions. In the legislative body, the General Synod, women are better represented than in Parliament. They form 10% of the total membership of the General Synod, and 23% of the House of Laity within that body. However, they are not well represented on committees. There are no women at all on the doctrinal or legislative committees. Women make up only 5.8% of the Board of Finance, and 6% of the Standing Committee. There are only 2.5% of women among the Church Commissioners. Yet women make up at least 60% of the active membership of the Church as judged by the 60/40 ratio of women/men who are confirmed members.[17]

The British Council of Churches, an ecumenical body, has only 14.4% of women on its central council. At world level, the pattern is similar. At the Uppsala Assembly of the World Council of Churches, which met in 1968, only 9% of the delegates were women. The programme staffs and committees of the World Council of Churches are predominantly male.[18]

The position of women varies greatly in other religious cultures. Mohammedans only permit their women to stand behind the men at worship. Women are segregated from men in Orthodox Jewish synagogues. Women do not count towards the necessary quorum for worship. Hindu women do not take an active part in the official temple worship, although they have important roles to play in the religious rituals of their households. In all cultures, where women and men are members of the same religious sect, women play little part as leaders.*

In this chapter I have focused on some of the more obvious effects of sexism on people's lives. These facts make sombre, and perhaps familiar, reading, but I do not think that we should allow the all-pervasive unpleasantness of sexism to cloud our sense of humour. Sexism has a funny side to it, which highlights its absurdity. Those of us who are its victims need to be able to laugh at it, and at ourselves. I can still remember the moment when my own sense of humour burst through my sense of outrage at being treated as a 'non-person' in the Church.

During my 3½ years of theological training, I was the only woman among 45 students. Our principal was kindness itself. He included me in every activity. Yet for 3½ years he called me 'brother'. Three years ago, I went to a Church conference where 50 of the 500 delegates were women. The Bishop unfailingly addressed us all as 'brothers'. On this occasion I protested. Some months later, I had accumulated a collection of letters, which had arrived from our Diocesan office. They were all correctly addressed, but inside each letter began 'Dear brother'. I had repeatedly suggested that the word 'sister' could have been included, but without success. Then one day I looked at the latest letter. It was still uncompromisingly addressed, 'Dear brother'. I began

* In Britain all organised religious bodies are totally exempted from the Sex Discrimination Bill (1975).

C

to feel irritated as usual, and then suddenly I saw the funny side of the situation. I was irritated because I felt that my womanhood was being ignored; but no form of address, however incorrect, could make me less of a woman than I knew myself to be. The people who kept address-ing me as though I was a man were probably unaware of their apparent insensitivity. I laughed aloud, and at that moment saw a way of helping them to understand. I wrote back to the clergyman who had written to me. The letter began, 'Dear sister', and it ended, 'Your brother Una'. Since then, I have sometimes used the generic term 'sister' when talking to an audience of men. The results of such actions have been splendid! This gentle and humorous activity has been my way of asking that my sex be recognised as an important part of my humanity. It is a very small courtesy to ask for, but it is very hard to achieve, for it asks for a revolution in thought and language.

Since I have discovered my sense of humour, I have found that it has helped me to preserve a sense of proportion about sexism. Humour and common sense, however, have not obliterated my belief that sexism is a serious social disease. While I recognise the fact that some families and some societies manage to live without becoming tainted by the systematic subordination of either sex to the other, I know that the evidence shows that women are usually treated as the subordinates of men. Many women still believe that in reality they are inferior to men. Other women believe that they are not men's inferiors, but their superiors. Men are similarly ambivalent in their beliefs. More-over, I know that sexism could not exist at all in social institutions unless it was acceptable to the majority of women and men who make up society.

It is, therefore, important to look beyond the facts about sexism to the roots of the problem. Here I acknowledge that there are impor-tant historical, political, sociological, anthropological and religious roots to sexism. These fields are already well covered by existing litera-ture. In the present study I am concentrating on a more existential approach in which the psychology of sexism is important. In the next chapter I intend to focus attention on to those attitudes of women and men which make the oppression of one group by the other possible.

2 The psychology of sexism

'Men are as oppressed as women.'
(Mme R. R. Andriamanjato, chief water engineer, Madagascar)

Some years ago we were at a dinner party. The Equal Pay Act, giving women and men in Britain equal basic pay for equal work, had just been passed. The conversation turned to what this Act might mean for the future relations between the sexes.

'Well, I for one won't stand for it in my firm,' said one of the party. 'I'll find my way round the Act. I don't believe in all your "women's lib" ideas, as you know,' he said, turning to me.

'Tell me why you feel so strongly about it,' I said.

'I will,' he replied. 'It will destroy family life if women ever bring home more money than their husbands. I know I'd feel absolutely disgraced as a man if my wife earned more than I do. I wouldn't let her go out to work anyway,' he added.

I have heard this sort of argument many times in my life. There is a deep fear behind such a statement. Some men feel that their financial superiority in the home is closely tied up with their role as head of the household. They think that authority is part of their manhood, and so when their authority is threatened their masculinity is also threatened. Some of them, like my friend, restrict the lives of their wives in order to ensure that their dependants are never in a position to challenge their masculinity. They will try to limit the pay of women in their employ for the same reason.

It is fairly easy for women like myself to pin the label of 'male chauvinist pig' on to men who deliberately keep us subordinate to themselves, in order to preserve their own sense of self-esteem. We can so easily come to feel that we are imprisoned in restricted roles without good reason. We begin to hate our prison bars, and we learn to hate the men who have the power to keep the prison gates shut. We are tempted to try to force our way through the barriers, and to see men as our chief enemies. There is a certain bitter satisfaction in hurling ourselves against sexist attitudes and structures even when they do not yield to our attack. It is also easier to fight men, whom we can see as obvious enemies, than to fight an unknown enemy which lurks deep within ourselves as well as outside ourselves. I certainly reacted with this kind of destructive anger when I first became aware of the restricting effects of sexism on women's lives. Later, I came to realise that men can be as much imprisoned in their 'superior' roles as women are in their 'inferior' ones. I had to admit that such a persistent disease as sexism merited a more radical analysis than I had originally thought. I began to redirect my energies so as to try to understand more about the roots of the disease.

I had not progressed very far with my investigations when, one day, I went to listen to a theologian who was explaining why he thought that women were inferior in their being to men. As soon as this learned clergyman had stated his thesis, I felt myself beginning to bridle at the way in which he was using the term 'inferior'. He was talking in rather dry, theoretical terms about the ontological inferiority of women. His lack of emotion about the whole subject, coupled with his apparent indifference to the plight of some of the women whom he so neatly consigned to an inferior category, provoked me into opposition. I noticed that I was responding to the whole concept of inferiority with the firm conviction that it was bad for anyone to have to be in an inferior position, though I conceded that people had a right to choose such a position if they wanted to. I was well aware that some of the women in the audience accepted their inferior status with equanimity. I knew that some women, as well as men, genuinely supported the theologian's arguments about the ontological inferiority of women, although at the same time they thought that social equality between the sexes was a matter of justice. I could appreciate that some people felt that women were so superior to men that they deserved to be put on pedestals and kept there. These varied points of view were all voiced in questions after the lecture. Our discussions left me feeling more confused than before about the whole subject of being human. I sensed, however, that my confusion contained important clues to the psychological origins of sexism, provided I could unravel these clues from their emotional overtones, and check them against other people's experiences. This single incident encouraged me to undertake a serious study of the psychology of sexism. In doing this work, I paid special attention to the ways in which inferiority feelings contribute to the development of sexist attitudes. I also studied the origins of inferiority feelings themselves.

The development of inferiority feelings in individuals

Children are not born with an inherent sense of their own worth. They acquire this from their parents. In their pre-school years children are very sensitive to emotional atmosphere. They quickly learn that some of their personality traits are more acceptable than others to their parents, or to other parental figures. They learn to associate parental approval of themselves and of their behaviour with feelings of happiness, and parental rejection of any kind with unhappiness. All parents make use of these feelings of happiness and unhappiness in the training and upbringing of the children. Children, therefore, tend to behave in such a way as to win their parents' approval, and to keep their affections. When they go against their parents' wishes they experience an unhappy separation from them which they feel as guilt. This guilt induces them to seek a restoration to parental approval. The sense of guilt also lowers them in their own eyes, so that they feel inferior both to their 'good' selves and to their parents and others. They regain some of their self-esteem when they are accepted back by their parents. All children pass through this moulding process, which leaves permanent marks on their characters. Parental likes and dislikes, their concepts of right and wrong, become incorporated into the consciences of their children, where they continue to influence the subsequent attitudes and actions of the children, even when they become adults.

Very young children notice that they are different in many ways from others, but they do not make value judgements about these differences. It is only when they learn to attach values to their differences that children realise that some people are treated as if they were more valuable and more approved of than others. Children learn to evaluate the differences between themselves and others, in the first place from their parents, and later on from other children and adults. They unconsciously absorb the feelings and attitudes of their parents and others, whose approval they desire, towards a variety of characteristics in other people, such as race, sex, education, financial status, religion and morality.

Once children learn to make value judgements, they begin to compare themselves with others. They soon learn that they can excel over other children in some respects. Those who excel are often praised by their parents, and develop pride in their achievements. Those who do not do so well sense their parents' disappointment, and often feel miserable. Children compete with each other for their parents' and teachers' approval. This competitiveness is frequently encouraged in the educational system. Success or failure reinforces emergent feelings of superiority or inferiority. At this stage of development, when the child is at school, partial failure can be interpreted as total failure. Many children, for instance, are so sensitive about their lack of achievement that they may need to be strongly reassured by their parents and teachers, so that they do not feel that their failure at examinations means that they are failures as people.

In adolescence, inferiority feelings usually spread beyond achievement to include personal characteristics. In particular, young people are very vulnerable about their emergent sexuality. The lives of young women and men can become tortured by feelings of inferiority and sexual inadequacy. In this way, a young woman can suffer emotional agony because she has small breasts, and an adolescent youth can feel that he will be inadequate as a man because he has a small penis.

Most adults try to adjust to the realities of life by coping with their inevitable feelings of inferiority and superiority in socially acceptable ways. Superiority feelings can find legitimate expression in family and work achievements, but inferiority feelings are much harder to deal with because they often have their origins in unhappy childhood experiences. For example, many people have suffered the humiliation of feeling foolish in front of a lot of other children when they failed to answer a teacher's question. The experience was so traumatic for some of them that they repressed the unhappy memory; in effect they have forgotten it. All that remains with them is a vague sense of uneasiness whenever they are asked to speak in public. Some people who are afflicted in this way may even refuse invitations to speak to a group of people on subjects about which they know a considerable amount. They are afraid of making fools of themselves, and, though they do not know why they feel this, it is often because their childhood experience still actively influences their adult behaviour.

Although human beings remain individuals they cannot live in isolation from one another. They are always learning from others and from experience. Ideas and feelings are infectious and spread within communities. They are handed down from generation to generation. They are preserved in the structures of societies by tradition.

The spread of inferiority feelings to certain groups in society

In every community there are groups of people who share certain characteristics with each other. There are, for instance, fat people and thin ones, tall and short people, black and white ones. There are women and men, some of whom are heterosexual while others are homosexual. Each group, in each pair, has a particular and distinctive characteristic which distinguishes it from its opposite in the pair. In each pair the distinctions between the characteristics are so definite that it becomes easy to separate one group from another.

This easy differentiation between people according to their shape, size, colour of skin, gender or sexual orientation makes it simple for inferiority feelings to attach themselves to one or other of the groups in each pair. People may feel themselves to be inferior because they are thin or fat, tall or short. The choice is arbitrary : what matters in this context is that one group or the other submits to those in the opposite group. People who feel inferior act as if they were inferior : those who feel superior act as if they were superior.

In time, a social consensus may develop in which it becomes accepted that a particular characteristic confers inferior status on the person or group which possesses that characteristic. In this way it comes to be taken for granted that black people are inferior to white people, homosexuals are inferior to heterosexuals and women are inferior to men. These ideas spread to other communities. They are taught to children. They become part of history. After generations of education it is common to find that many of the so-called inferior people take their own inferiority as a matter of course.

This unconscious acceptance of inferior status is illustrated by an episode which occurred within the past two years. A firm advertised for a woman executive and offered a high salary for the post. There were no applicants. A few weeks later the same job was re-advertised at an annual salary a thousand pounds less than before. This time the firm received many applications from highly qualified women. When they were asked why they had not applied before some of the women said that they did not feel they were sufficiently well qualified for such a highly paid post. It was pointed out to them that they were already doing equivalent work : what had been offered was parity with men in the same grade of work. These women had become used to their sex-linked salary differential. At a deep level of personality they had accepted a belief that they were not worth as much pay as men. They were conditioned to feel comfortable in their inferior status.

The need for status in an organised society

A concept of status is only possible because human beings believe that they have to live in a structured society if they are to live in harmony with each other rather than in chaos.

People grow into a particular structure of organised community, and they teach their children to fit into their families and into their societies by teaching them the rules of the communities to which they belong. They encourage their children to obey lawful authority. They carry out their training by a process of social conditioning, and by explaining to their children why the rules are necessary.

Young children usually obey their parents and other adults because they need to feel accepted. Their submission to the superior strength and authority of older people is one way of ensuring that they are acceptable to them. As children grow older the approval of other children comes to mean more to them than the approval of parents. At this stage, they are often willing to risk losing the love of their parents for the sake of their friends. By the time they are adolescents many of them rebel against their parents. When their parents disapprove of their behaviour they can retaliate by rejecting parental authority. When they are made to feel inferior to other people they compensate for the humiliation by acting defiantly, as if they were very superior to the adults whom they oppose. Most adults have a need to feel accepted by the societies in which they live. They therefore modify their behaviour to suit the situations in which they find themselves. This process of social adaptation continues throughout life.

All structured societies work upon the principle that some members must remain inferior if others are to be their superiors and govern them. This principle works well in the family unit during the years when the children are immature and dependent upon adults. In adult society, however, all the members are potential parents. If the same principle of government by authority is to be maintained, it becomes necessary to choose some people to be superiors and others to remain their inferiors.

The choice of who is to remain subordinate and who is to govern can be made according to the individual abilities of the people who make up the community. In practice, however, the choice is seldom made on such sensible criteria. Instead, people are put into groups according to characteristics which are easily distinguishable. The status of the individuals who make up any particular group is defined by the status of the group to which they belong. This makes it easy to define who is to be superior and who is to be inferior. It simplifies the selection procedures when it comes to the choice of who is to govern and who is to obey. When the demarcation lines between people in different groups are very clear the choice is that much easier. For instance, it is much simpler to group people into black and white than it is to group them into rich and poor. In all societies the most obvious demarcation is that which divides women from men.

The physical differences between women and men are so obvious that it has always been easy for women and men to feel that the superior size and strength of men must mean that men were superior to women in other ways, even in their essential being. Men also have been free from the repetitive work of child-bearing, and so it has been relatively easy for them to assume the reins of government. Women have been expected to be obedient to men at home as well as in society, although at times women have had to be subjugated by physical force, and at times they have successfully rebelled against men. In modern society some of our attitudes to the physical differences between women and men have changed, but in many communities women are still treated as though they were inferior to men, although few people now like openly to admit to this belief.

The external subjugation of women, and their relegation in society, does not matter as much as the kind of inferiority feelings which develop in people of both sexes because of the internal images they have of what they ought to be like as feminine women or masculine men. I can best illustrate what I mean by looking at the kinds of social conditioning which are usual in Western society. In general, women and men are still trained for different roles. Women are expected to be passive, receptive, gentle, good and unselfish. Girls are rewarded whenever their behaviour conforms to this pattern. Men are expected to be active, thrusting, forceful, ambitious and dominant. Boys are rewarded when they comply with this expectation. Unorthodox behaviour is strongly discouraged by repeated instructions like 'Little girls don't fight' and 'Little boys don't cry'. As adults, women and men are encouraged to keep within their socially acceptable roles by a similar system of rewards and punishments. For example, a woman who behaves in a 'feminine' way is praised for being a 'real' woman : a man who behaves in a 'masculine' way is praised for being a 'real' man. Any woman who steps outside her role and, for instance, acts aggressively, immediately risks being described as 'a mannish creature who wants to wear the trousers' : similarly, any man who acts in a gentle way risks being called 'an old woman'.

There are two psychological mechanisms at work in these kinds of situation. In the first place, women and men both defend themselves against inferiority feelings by appropriating certain qualities to their own sex. These qualities become 'superior' ones so long as they are exhibited by members of the same sex. In this way a very 'superior' woman is someone who displays all the qualities which she and society have labelled as 'feminine' : a very 'superior' man is one who shows an abundance of 'masculine' qualities. This defensive mechanism enables women and men not to feel inferior as human beings, provided that they do not step outside the accepted limits of behaviour for their own sex. In the second place, women and men are able to admire qualities like aggressiveness and gentleness without ranking them in order of merit, provided that they see them only in the opposite sex; they would despise the same qualities if they discovered them in themselves. This explains why some women admire ambition in men, but do not like to see it in themselves, or in other women : men can admire tenderness in women, but often feel it to be a sign of weakness in themselves.

I have heard sincere men say that 'women are far superior to men', while at the same time they are taking good care to keep women in subordinate positions at work. In the same way, I have heard women say, 'Of course, men are superior to women', while they are treating their husbands at home as if they were unfit to have charge of the kitchen, the housekeeping money or the children. This kind of 'double-think', which allows people to say one thing and do another, is a familiar defence mechanism which everyone uses at times.

The psychological mechanisms which I have described allow people to accept their status in a sexist society without losing their self-respect as individuals. Sexism is a subtle evil. The injustice of using sexual criteria to determine social status is obscured when people are conditioned into separate roles, and are then given 'superior' status in their own group only if they excel in those qualities which are designated to be 'masculine' or 'feminine'.

The first section of this chapter has been concerned with the place of inferiority feelings in the processes of socialisation to which people are exposed throughout their lives. Social conditioning is an important factor in the development and reinforcement of sexism in society. Sexism appears to be the most tenacious of all the discriminatory evils. such as racism, extreme nationalism or any other chauvinism. Sexism could not have such a strong hold on society as it does, unless it had roots within the basic structure of the human personality.

The next section of this chapter is, therefore, concerned with the ways in which individual women and men react to their internal experiences of inferiority. It also looks at some theories as to why women and men react as they do to interior stress between different parts of their personalities.

Everyone is born with a unique genetic constitution, and into different circumstances. Human beings depend both upon their inheritance and upon the environment with which they interact. This interaction differs from person to person. For instance, inferiority feelings are universal among human beings and, potentially, there are as many different ways of reacting to them as there are people. The work of many observers, however, has shown that human beings react in broadly similar ways to each other : this means that it is possible to discern several patterns of reaction to internal feelings of inferiority.

Patterns of reaction to internal feelings of inferiority

Feelings of inferiority are very closely linked with feelings of insecurity. If people feel that they are not worthwhile, they often feel that they are unlovable. They doubt that their parents could love them, and so they become unsure of themselves. Many people manage to fight their feelings of inferiority and insecurity : they achieve a kind of equitable compromise between feeling inferior in some respects and worthwhile in others. Some of them lose the battle, and become the victims of their inferiority feelings in one of two ways. A number of people submit to their feelings of inferiority and become oppressed by them. Others fight their inferiority feelings so hard that they go to the opposite extreme, and become unable to admit to themselves or to anyone else that they are inferior in any respect. These two different ways of reacting to the same problem are well illustrated by two examples taken from life. The identities of the people concerned are composite ones.

Jack had always been timid. He was the third child in a family of five. As a small boy he hardly ever left his mother's side. Of all her children, he was the only one whom she had to force to go to school. Jack hated school, mainly because he felt that he was always being picked upon by the teachers. His school reports always said, 'This boy could do better if he tried harder.' There were always rows at home over these reports. His parents and teachers knew that he was intelligent, but Jack insisted that he did not have the abilities that his brothers and sisters had. They were all at the same school and were all successful and popular. Jack however, was successful neither at work nor at games, and was too shy to make many friends.

Jack left school without passing any examinations. He went to work in a shoe shop where he did quite well, being punctual, conscientious and hard working. He never married, but continued to live at home.

When the manager of the shoe shop retired Jack was offered the job. He took it because of the increased wages. Although the job was well within his capability, Jack worried about the responsibility. He found it difficult to manage the junior staff. One of the younger men, with little experience, seemed to have brilliant ideas about display, which made Jack feel inadequate and old-fashioned.

After a year, Jack had a nervous breakdown. His doctors advised him to take a job with less responsibility. He came back to the shop to find his young rival in the manager's position. Jack never even asked for a transfer to another shop. He accepted his subordinate position without a murmur of protest.

Jack had responded to internal feelings of inferiority by accepting them as reality. Despite many good qualities, much love and help from his family, and some good chances in life, Jack's personality was such that he felt inferior, he acted as if he was inferior, and in the end he was treated in the same way.

Anthony was just as timid as Jack, but for some reason he was more afraid of his parents' displeasure than of anything else in the world. He needed to please them at any cost, so he hid his fear when he went to school.

Anthony was determined to prove himself a success. He worked very hard and never spared himself. He had to struggle to pass his examinations, but he managed to get to university and became a doctor.

Anthony never became a specialist. Instead, he joined a good practice as a family doctor. He married and had two children. He was as stern with his children as he thought his parents had been with him. His wife rebelled against his authoritarian behaviour towards her and the children, and she left him after ten years of marriage.

Anthony continued to work hard and, in time, he became the senior partner of the firm. He was very kind to some patients, but treated others, who dared to challenge his authority, as if they were fools. He was also very hard on his junior colleagues, and for this reason he never retained their services for very long. The only doctors he could get as locums were those who were willing to be subservient because of their own inadequacies. Until he retired, Anthony blamed everyone else for his misfortunes and never saw how he himself had contributed to them.

Anthony had responded to his inferiority feelings by over-reacting against them. He had become the kind of person who was so insecure that he could not admit that he might be wrong. In order to maintain his own self-respect he had tried to keep his wife and children under control. He had had to keep his patients and partners subordinate to himself at all costs.

Jack and Anthony shared the same problems; they reacted to it in different ways. Both of them became the servants of compulsive elements in their own personalities. They could only retain some sense of security by submerging themselves in the roles they had created for themselves. People like Jack tend to become the subordinate members of any society, and people like Anthony tend to become the dominant, authoritarian people in the community.

The examples which I have chosen were both men. They might equally well have been women. Inferiority feelings attach themselves to personality traits rather than to the sexuality of their victims. However, it is true that it is more usual for women to be found among the oppressed groups in a society, and for men to be found among their oppressors. In part, this sex-linked difference is undoubtedly due to the effects of social conditioning, but the fact also raises the question as to whether there is any deep-rooted difference in the way in which women and men respond to internal inferiority feelings which would account for the way in which they seem to gravitate towards one extreme or the other.

Some theories as to why women accept subordinate
status more easily than men

I have already outlined the ways by which psychological role conditioning conspires with physical and sociological differences between women and men to consign women to an inferior role in society, and men to the superior role of government. Both these roles restrict the full development of personality.

In the nineteenth century, some alternative theories were advanced by three psychiatrists who became very influential in Western society. These men sought to understand why people behave as they do. They then propounded theories to explain what they had observed. Their theories are still influential today.

Sigmund Freud (1856–1939) believed that women were biologically inferior to men. He thought that women felt inferior to men because they knew that they lacked the external genitalia of which men were so proud. Freud believed that little girls suffered from 'penis envy'. According to him, when young girls discovered that they did not have male organs they transferred their love away from their defective mothers to their fathers, and later to their husbands, in the hope of compensating for their own lack of virility. For the same reason, Freud held that mothers took a special pleasure in bearing sons.

Freud thought that small boys felt themselves to be the rivals of their fathers for their mothers' affections. When they found that women did not have external genitalia, they were afraid of being castrated if they persisted in their rivalry with their fathers. The fear of castration immediately caused young boys to repress their incestuous love for their mothers and their hostilities towards their fathers. In this way, boys identified with their fathers and took on their dominant roles. According to classical Freudian theory, a woman is feminine only when she fully accepts her biological, passive and receptive role : a man is masculine only when he accepts his active and dominant role.

I have mentioned these well-known theories precisely because they are so widely remembered. This fact typifies the way in which sexists can build their own theories upon the partial teaching of an influential person without taking cognisance of his environment. A later psychoanalyst, Dr Clara Thompson, pointed this out when she said :

> Freud was a very perceptive thinker but he was a male, and a male quite ready to subscribe to the theories of male superiority prevalent in the culture. This must have definitely hampered his understanding of experience in a woman's life, especially those specifically associated with her feminine role.[1]

Freud himself acknowledged that he did not understand what women wanted, and he also said :

Psychoanalysis does not try to describe what a woman is – that would be a task it could scarcely perform – but sets about enquiring how she comes into being, how a woman develops out of a child with a bisexual disposition.[2]

Freud's theories are sometimes used by present-day sexists to reinforce their own views about women without their taking note of the work of later analysts within his own school, like Ernest Jones, Karen Horney and Frieda Fromm-Reichmann, who disagreed with some of his theories about women.

Alfred Adler (1870–1937) was at one time a pupil and colleague of Freud. Whereas Freud always explained people's behaviour in terms of the influence of their past experiences on their present behaviour, Adler thought about the effects of people's hopes for the future on their immediate behaviour.

Initially, Adler focused on organ inferiority. He postulated a theory that an individual adjusted to organ inferiority by compensating for the deficiency either within the organ itself, or within other organs, or through compensatory psychological adjustments. In practice, this theory meant that a man who was deficient in height or strength could compensate for his inferiority in these respects by developing his intelligence or cunning, and so remain self-confident, or even become dominant over other men. Later, Adler laid less emphasis on organ inferiority and paid more attention to the effects of social inferiority on people's lives.

Adler stressed the importance of aggressive drives in the development of personality. He taught that aggression could be sublimated, or displaced, into socially useful occupations such as law, medicine, preaching or teaching. Aggression could also be transformed into excessive weakness, so that inadequate people could use their weakness as a form of emotional blackmail to dominate other people.

In Adler's time, men were thought to be more naturally aggressive than women, At one time, Adler attached superiority to the 'masculine' trait of aggression. He also equated superiority with masculinity and inferiority with femininity. He taught that both women and men compensated for feelings of inferiority by striving to become more adequate, and he felt that everyone, women as well as men, really wanted to be male. Adler said that on occasion very insecure people could counteract their inferiority feelings by acting in an overbearing manner and generally behaving as if they were very superior human beings instead of very insecure ones who felt themselves to be inferior. He also felt that neurotic women rejected their feminine role through a 'masculine protest' and this influenced them to enter 'masculine' professions such as engineering, business or medicine.

These theories about inferiority and superiority are what most people remember about Adler's teaching, because they fit neatly into the kind of psychology which sexism feeds on. It is therefore all the more important to remember that at a later date, when Adler had formulated his ideas about individual psychology still further, he could write :

> If our civilization is marked by a prejudice, then this prejudice reaches out and touches every aspect of that civilization, and is to be found in its every manifestation. The fallacy of the inferiority of women, and its corollary, the superiority of man, constantly disturbs the harmony of the sexes. As a result, an unusual tension is introduced into all erotic relationships, thereby threatening, and often entirely annihilating, every chance for happiness between the sexes.[3]

Carl Jung (1870–1961) pointed out that since each human being was formed from the union of a woman with a man, each human being contained elements of the feminine and masculine within his biological and psychological make-up. Jung held that there was a balance of femininity and masculinity within each individual's personality.

According to Jung, each woman had a conscious 'persona' which was feminine : at the unconscious level she had a masculine part to her personality which Jung called her 'animus'. Conversely, each man had a conscious 'persona', which was masculine, and in his unconscious, a feminine part, the 'anima'. Jung held that when a woman was closely identified with her feminine 'persona', she achieved this at the expense of her 'animus', for she had to keep the masculine elements of her personality well submerged. The converse would apply to men. Jung believed that the submerged elements of the personality could act autonomously, so as to influence a person's behaviour.

Jung's theories about personality held that femininity and masculinity coexisted in one person in a way which did not require the polarisation of these two into separate people of different sex. Like Freud and Adler he still assumed that certain personality traits were sex-linked. He thought that usually there would be a struggle between the two sides of a person's personality so that the 'persona', or 'front', of a person could always be presened to the outside world in an acceptable way. Only if people were aware of the hidden facets of their personalities could they hope to integrate them into one whole person. Jung left us a clear portrait of his idea of a 'whole' person when he wrote a eulogy of one of his friends. This man, who had recently died, was Richard Wilhelm. He was a student and scholar who had studied the Chinese way of life. He had made a fine translation of the *I Ching*. Jung wrote :

As a rule the specialist's is a purely masculine mind and intellect to which fecundity is an alien and unnatural process; it is therefore an especially ill-adapted tool for giving rebirth to a foreign spirit. But a larger mind bears the stamp of the feminine; it is endowed with a receptive and fruitful womb which can reshape what is strange and give it a familiar form. Wilhelm possessed the rare gift of a maternal intellect. To it he owed his unequalled ability to feel his way into the spirit of the East and to make his imcomparable translations.[4]

The theories of these three men have conditioned the thoughts and emotions of women and men over the past hundred years. They have strongly reinforced the idea that certain characteristics are linked with one or other of the sexes. They have moulded public opinion to such an extent that people actually changed their behaviour to fit into the theoretical structures which supported sex-linking. For many generations, Western women were afraid to express any 'masculine' feelings, lest they be accused of being neurotically masculine, and men dared not show any 'feminine' traits lest they should be accused of being too womanly. Abraham Maslow writes of these fears :

The antagonism between the sexes is largely a projection of the unconscious struggle within the person, between his or her masculine and feminine components. The man who is fighting within himself all the qualities he and his culture define as feminine will fight these same qualities in the external world, especially if his culture values maleness more than femaleness as is so often the case. If it be emotionality, or dependency, or love, or colours, or tenderness with babies he will be afraid of these in himself. He will fight them in the external world and try to be opposite. And he will fight them in the external world too by rejecting them, by relegating them to women entirely.[5]

D

It is surely relevant that as the influence of these three great psychologists has waned in Western society, or been diluted by other theories about the nature of personality, such as the Gestalt and Behaviourist schools of psychology, the fortunes of women in society have improved. It is noticeable that in countries which were relatively uninfluenced by analytical theories, but heavily influenced by Pavlovian ideas, women have been more often treated as equal to men than in other societies. Religious and political ideologies are intimately influenced by psychological theories, and in turn they influence the development of psychology so that the interaction affects people's external lives and also their personalities. In a wider context Winston S. Churchill summarised this interplay in the phrase : 'We shape our buildings, and afterwards our buildings shape us.'[6]

This chapter has only been concerned with the psychology of sexism. Psychology can explain why some people feel inferior to others, and how society can organise inferiority feelings so that they can be used to perpetuate social structures in which women and men play separate and different roles from each other, and in which women are usually subordinate to men. Psychology can also help people to realise that oppressors and oppressed share a common problem of how to live with their own deep-rooted sense of insecurity.

In a sexist society life can be quite comfortable for some people, for they can allay their sense of insecurity by conforming to their assigned roles. Roles, however, force people to play-act. They are no longer able to be fully themselves, for the real self becomes subordinated to the role which the person has to assume. Sexism constrains individuality. It prevents people from seeing what women and men really are, or might become, and it conceals from them their potential for a real relationship with each other.

The psychology of sexism does not reveal much about the true psychology of sexuality or human personality. At the end of this chapter I find myself knowing a bit more about why sexism has been so successful in distorting the lives of women and men. I am conscious that I have not yet begun to discuss the nature of humanity, nor of true femaleness or maleness. This then must be the next task if people are to see why the sexist structures of society should be changed to allow the development of a more just and true relationship between women and men.

3 Becoming aware of our humanity

'It is the capacity to accept what I am which makes me human.'
(Fr Harry Williams, C.R., 1970)

I am sometimes tempted to think that the very existence of the human species is the most powerful argument against the existence of God. I have only to look at the broken body of a battered child to be reminded of Dostoevsky's passionate novel, *The Brothers Karamazov*, in which he asks his most searching question, in the words of Ivan, who asks Aloysha :

> Imagine that you are creating a fabric of human destiny with the object of making men happy in the end, giving them peace and rest at last, but that it was essential and inevitable to torture to death only one tiny creature – that baby beating its breast with its fist, for instance – and to found that edifice on its tears; would you consent to be architect on these conditions?[1]

In the book, Aloysha replies : 'No, I couldn't consent.' Most people would probably give the same answer. The human mind shrinks from the thought of having to be the kind of God who could be capable of creating human beings who can deliberately torture helpless children, or kill each other over a prolonged period with the refined skills of modern torture and weapons of war.

At an intellectual level, it may be possible to arrive at a satisfactory philosophical answer as to why a loving God should make human beings who are capable of such behaviour. At an existential level, when I have been confronted with the anguish of a terrified child, or the suffering of a parent whose son has been slowly tortured to death by his fellow men, I have never found the philosophical or theological arguments at all relevant. In these kinds of situation, words have been useless as vehicles for the anguished cry of the human heart, which asks,

'Why are human beings as they are?' The cynic in me reminds me that human beings are the only animals who kill their own kind for pleasure. The idealist in me recalls the superb achievements of people – their discoveries, their art, their love and tenderness for each other. The realist that I am accepts that both the cynic and the idealist are right in their assessment of human nature, and also acknowledges my own share in the guilt and glory of my human condition.

I cannot pretend to understand why a loving God should have created such a contradictory creature as a human being. Perhaps, therefore, I should pay attention to Alexander Pope's famous injunction :

> Know then thyself, presume not God to scan,
> The proper study of Mankind is Man.[2]

'Mankind' has never lacked people who have spent their whole lives as students of human nature. They have left their reflections on record. Yet today, when I set out to define what a human being is I still find myself up against a seemingly impossible task. I can say what a human being is made of. I can even begin to understand how the various constituents of the human body are put together. I can look at the chromosomal patterns of women and men, and predict with reasonable certainty what diseases and congenital abnormalities they might pass on to their offspring if they marry. I know a great deal about how human beings behave, and why they behave as they do. I know all this because of the work done by my predecessors. Yet I find that I know scarcely anything about how it is possible for human beings to be able to remember, think, choose, create and worship, nor do I know why they do these things.

The task of discovering what human beings are is made more difficult because knowledge advances at such a rapid rate. This means that people who are students of human nature, and who are themselves caught up in the dynamic processes of evolution, are always having to re-assess their theories, and the theories themselves are in a continual state of flux. For instance, it used to be thought that there were certain features about human beings which distinguished them from all other animals. It was thought that only human beings used tools, that only human beings could think, that only people could plant and harvest crops. It is now known that chimpanzees in the wild have been seen to use primitive tools, without having been taught to do so by human beings : that they can be taught to play 'noughts and crosses' with people, and can often defeat their opponents.[3] The ecologists have discovered that there are over one hundred species of ants in the New World which can cultivate and harvest crops. Ant communities plan for the future by stockpiling food. They herd aphids to milk them of honeydew. They farm mushroom gardens within underground nests. They communicate with each other through chemical transmitters which are passed from one ant to another in a sort of 'kiss' called rophallaxis. Like human beings, they even kill their own kind, but apparently not for pleasure, although as yet there is no precise way of monitoring the emotions of ants.[4] In recent years ecologists, ethologists and anthropologists have made considerable advances towards a better understanding of the place of human beings within the animal world of which they are a part. Scientists are well used to seeing theories which were valid only a few years or decades ago overthrown by new discoveries or explanations which fit the observed facts better than the old hypotheses. They are accustomed to using any good theory as a stepping stone to the next discovery, or revelation of the truth.

If the speed of scientific discovery makes it difficult for an individual student to reach a satisfactory conclusion about who and what a human being is, then the slow, deliberate pace of theological and philosophical speculation constitutes a difficulty in the opposite direction. Theologians and philosophers interest themselves in human beings, not so much to find out what they are and how they work, but to discover why they exist, and how they have come to be what they are in the world. Some of the greatest thinkers in history have used only a few words to define human beings, but they have chosen their words very carefully. For instance, in the fourth century before Christ, Aristotle gave history this definition 'Man, a reasoning animal.' By the twentieth century after the death of Christ, Teilhard de Chardin had significantly expanded that statement to 'Man, a reflective animal.' The change may have been slow : it is, however, indicative of a considerable change in approach.

Scientific speed and theological slow motion can serve truth better if they are allowed to stay together in tension with each other, than if they both proceed at their own pace in separation. There have been times in history, however, when they have appeared to part company altogether, and this has sometimes happened because of a misunderstanding of the function of each discipline. For instance, when Yuri Gagarin returned from outer space and declared that he had not seen God 'out there', he was making a scientific statement which could have had no theological consequence, since theologians had never expected that an infinite God could be located in visible space. Similarly, in the history of Christianity, the Bible has been used as a scientific textbook on many occasions when people have attempted to prove or disprove some new scientific knowledge by reference to it.

During the twelve years that I have been engaged in a serious study about the nature of human beings and their relationships with each other, I have tried to look at human beings from many different viewpoints, including the religious ones. In that time, I have seen the Bible used in arguments in so many contradictory ways that I have come to the conclusion that although it is quite possible to use the Bible as a proof text to support almost any hypothesis, it is not in the interest of truth, scientific or theological, to do so. This is why, in my present study, I have not used the Bible either as a literal document of scientific fact, or as a document which contains static information which must enshrine theological truth for all time. I have such respect for the Bible that I do not intend to try to twist the Creation myths to make them fit known scientific facts, nor to twist factual evidence about the nature of creation to fit the Biblical myths, which, so far as I am concerned, reflect truth to successive generations of human beings in a dynamic rather than a static way. Personally, I have found that the only way to avoid falling into either trap is to eschew the use of the Bible as an analytic tool with which to solve current problems, or as a proof text to support or deny existential theories about the nature of women and men, theories which, I know only too well, are just stepping stones to the next theory or perception of truth.

If then, I hope to discover what it means to be a twentieth-century person, I have to try to distinguish those features which make human beings a distinct species within the animal kingdom.

Human beings are animals who think creatively

It is known that all animals can learn. Much learning is the result of behavioural conditioning: for instance, a dog will learn to keep away from fire; children learn to fear the pain of fire before they can reason. Animals other than human beings can certainly solve simple problems, but it is not known to what extent they can reason, for so much of the behaviour is the result of reflex conditioning. Communication between people and other animals is not yet precise enough to enable human beings to evaluate the thinking processes of non-human animals. It is, however, apparent that human beings are the only animals who have ever harnessed fire for their own use. They can cook, and use fuels in a whole variety of ways quite unknown to the rest of the animal kingdom.

Human beings are able to reason. They are able to reflect on what they already know. They can build on past knowledge. They can invent something entirely new. Among animals, they alone can think creatively.

Human beings are self-aware

Adult human beings are conscious of themselves as people who are separate entities. They have the ability to say 'I'. Human babies are born with immature nervous systems and do not have this capacity. As they grow, children become aware of other people and things outside themselves, long before they appear to be aware of their own individuality. When they begin to talk, children invariably speak about themselves in the third person, as if they were really someone else. It is only later, at an age which varies from child to child, that they can say, 'I'm going to do this', or 'I want that'. From that time, a child is always exploring what it means to be self-aware. That discovery is always made in relation to the 'otherness' of outside things or people. This is the 'I-it', 'I-thou' relationship which Martin Buber expounds so thoroughly.

Human beings can choose to escape their conditioning

Some scientists of today would claim that human beings are nothing more than machines. They would regard people as animals with self-programming, computer-like, complex brains. Few scientists, even if they are orthodox materialists, would deny that Paul Tillich was expressing a truth when he claimed that people become really human only at times of decision, when they exercise free will.[5] Human children are taught through social conditioning, and early imprinting is important to the development of habitual behaviour, but because they have some freedom to choose between options, they can decide to go against that early conditioning at any stage of their lives. For instance, I remember an intelligent and devout nun who was rendered helpless by her patho-

logical fear of moths. Her fear was the result of some childhood fright
which had conditioned her responses. She was eventually able to use
her free will to seek medical help for her illness, and so was able to be
freed from her humiliating condition.

Free will implies that human beings are responsible for their choices.
I believe this to be a fact, although I recognise that circumstances,
emotional factors and early childhood conditioning can limit a person's
freedom to exercise choice, and so reduce responsibility.

Human beings have historical memories

Animals are able to communicate with each other, and some of them,
like human beings, use elaborate and sophisticated methods, like sonic
and radar signals, meaningful noises, and spoken and written language.

Animals have individual memory. They also have ancestral memory,
as can be seen, for instance, in the atavistic behaviour of a dog which
turns itself round and round, as did its wild ancestors, before it settles
down to sleep. Memory serves all animals during their lifetimes, but so
far as is known, no other animals can leave records of themselves this
side of death except human beings, who do so through their art and
writing.

Since the end of the Old Stone Age, about 20,000 years ago, human
beings have left records of their activities through their cave paintings.
They also carved figures of animals and people, and made images of
their gods. About 7000 years ago the Sumerians of Mesopotamia in-
vented the use of pictographs, which later developed into writing.
People then had a way of communicating with each other at a distance,
and of transmitting their knowledge to future generations. History was
born.

Human beings are aware of mystery

To all intents and purposes, animals other than human beings do not
seem to question why they exist, nor how they ought to live. They seem
to have no concern about their ultimate destiny. On the other hand,
there is evidence that human beings have been concerned about their
very existence for at least 100,000 years. As a distinguished French-
American biologist, René Dubos, has said :

For approximately 100,000 years, human life has been identified not only with the use of fire, but also with shelter, clothing, tools, weapons, complex social structures, and with the practice of some form of magic or worship. The fact that burial was practiced during the Stone Age even by Neanderthal man, suggests some form of ultimate concern.[6]

Evidence provided by ancient burial furniture indicates that at least 7000 years before Christ, some people, notably the Egyptians, believed in survival beyond the grave.

From very early records of human existence it is known that people have treated life as a mystery, because they have found themselves unable to understand some aspects of life. Mystery arises out of what cannot be explained, and evokes reverence and awe. It calls forth worship. Human beings have worshipped 'beings' outside themselves from very early times. They have worshipped the forces of nature, the spirits of trees, stones and animals, even other people. They have worshipped powers whom they have called 'gods', or 'God', which seem to control their destinies from beyond the earthly sphere.

The sense of mystery goes beyond reason and evokes a response which is called faith. Faith is a necessary part of all humanness. Faith, a belief in powers or personalities which influence human lives, requires that people should be in a 'right' relationship with these objects of worship, in order to obtain their assistance, and to control them. This seems to be the basis for human morality.

Animals other than human beings can be conditioned to behave in certain ways, either by their own community or by outsiders, including human beings. Animals appear to have some 'conscience', or fear of being punished, if they misbehave, that is if they go against their conditioning. Human beings can be similarly conditioned, and some feelings of 'guilt' are undoubtedly due to this kind of conditioning, but this is not the sum total of human conscience. Because of their conscience, human beings are able to go beyond the demands of the law, or fear of punishment : their conscience will constrain them to do more than the law requires for the sake of that which they love and worship.

In the past men have believed that they possessed all these qualities, which I have described as human, in their fullness, but that somehow women were not fully human. This attitude is shown by Aristotle, who was so influential on later Christian thinkers, like Thomas Aquinas. Aristotle wrote :

The female is, as it were, a mutilated male . . . a sort of natural deficiency.

In a religious context, the Apochryphal literature of the Gnostics, which was written after the death of Christ, betrays the same attitude. The final fragment of the Gospel of Thomas illustrates this :

> Simon Peter said to them :
>> Let Mariheam go away from us,
>> for women are not worthy of life.
> Jesus said :
>> Lo, I will draw her
>> so that I will make her a man
>> so that she too may become a living spirit
>> which is like you men ;
>> for every woman who makes herself a man
>> will enter into the kingdom of heaven.[7]

Few people would now subscribe to either of these views, and as I have shown, I cannot find any human characteristic which is not found in women as well as in men. Yet among many people the feeling persists that if women are not subhuman they are at least so different from men by reason of their sex, that they must have different roles in life. It is therefore necessary to explore the part which sex has to play in the formation of character.

4 Sex and character

'I love man as my fellow.'
(Mary Wollstonecroft, 1972)

In October 1974 there was a General Election in Britain. At that election I stood for Parliament as a candidate for the 'Women's Rights Campaign', a newly formed political pressure group. By doing so, I and my colleagues created a precedent. We broke the rules of decent behaviour in a sexist society. As one of my outraged friends put it, when she was trying to dissuade me from campaigning, 'Women in politics have always prided themselves that they are politicians who happen to be women.' Another said, 'You'll fail, and make the women's movement a laughing stock.'

By normal standards, the campaign could be counted as a magnificent failure. The failure was real enough, for we succeeded in polling only 298 votes out of a total of over 46,000. The magnificent part of the failure lay in the manner of it, for people from all over the country supported the campaign. They sent money, came to help in person and tired themselves out by working, addressing envelopes and canvassing. The people who supported us in the constituency were often those who had the most to lose by doing so. In spite of that magnificent failure, the campaign was also a spectacular success. It was a success because a number of women 'came out of the back of the chorus', as one journalist put it, to stand up and be counted. In effect, they were saying, 'Women in politics ought to be women who happen to be politicians', that is to say that femaleness was more important than a person's political loyalties. It was a success because a number of men faced the inevitable scorn they attracted when they came to help us. They did so with courage and equanimity. The spectacular part of the success lay in the willingness of people to expose their own beliefs to the public gaze. No one could hide under the cover of a party political manifesto, a ready-made speech, an orthodox stand, or a familiar message. If we meant what we were saying we had to be prepared to make a spectacle of ourselves. We had to be ready to be laughed at as fools.

After the election was over, we spent some time looking at the questions which the campaign had raised. I am not concerned here with the political issues, nor with strategy and future policy, but with some human issues which our political intervention brought to our awareness.

During the campaign I had become aware of the uneasy feelings which my own activities had provoked in some people who knew me quite well. They were disquieted because, by standing at all, I had asserted that there was an intrinsic worth in my being a woman, a worth which I and others considered was as important as my intelligence, political philosophy or acumen. Yet it seemed to them that the action itself was 'unfeminine'. It felt too much like an Adlerian 'masculine protest'. It was my emphasis on my being a woman that they did not like, not my participation in politics.

Then, many people found the whole campaign disturbing because it was run by a group of women in a style which was unfamiliar to them, but which is familiar to those who have worked in the women's movement. All our decisions were made on a collective basis. Flexibility was its keynote. There was no hierarchical structure in the campaign. Outside observers found the system bewildering.

'Who's giving the orders round here,' asked one of my male friends who had come to help.

'No one,' he was told. 'Tell us what you want to do; and do what you can see needs doing.'

People found themselves puzzled as to whether our unusual way of working was a result of a political philosophy, or a 'feminine' way of doing things.

Finally, there were some people who felt that we had endangered the women's movement. They felt that political expediency had seduced us into compromise with the male-dominated structures of politics.

I am not at all surprised that people felt bewildered. The whole campaign was based on our belief that the conventional sex-linked roles of women and men should not be confused with the fundamental biological characteristics which differentiate women from men. Our attempt to separate these two types of differences necessarily confused and irritated people because it threatened them with a challenge to change the way they thought and felt about the roles of women and men.

Since the campaign, I have spent some time attempting to untangle the confusion. In attempting to explain what I mean in the above paragraph, I have, in what follows, made a semantic distinction by using the words 'feminine' and 'masculine' to denote characteristics which are conventionally sex-linked. For instance, many people feel that gentleness is a 'feminine' quality, and aggressiveness is a 'masculine' one – that is to say, they are linking personality characteristics with sex. By contrast, I have used 'female' and 'male' to denote biological sexual differences.

It is my personal belief that there are no personality characteristics which are linked with a particular sex, but that, because they are 'female' and 'male', women and men use human characteristics in different ways. I want to make it clear that I consider the concepts of 'feminine' and 'masculine' (femininity/masculinity) to be sexist in that they imprison human beings in sex-linked roles. I consider that 'female' and 'male' take account of the proper distinction between free women and men.

I do not think that this task of disentanglement is an easy one which can be solved immediately, or even in the near future, by one person. It is a task for many minds and many approaches. I believe that the task must be approached existentially as well as by rational, psychological and religious exploration. People must be content to travel slowly, groping for the answers, as they try to live out their partial solutions to the problems of relationships between women and men, in the hope of moving one step nearer to a more complete understanding of the nature of human personality.

At this stage it may be helpful to look at those features which separate women from men, and those which bring them together.

It is important to recognise that all human life starts as the result of the union of two highly specialised cells, the ovum and the sperm, but that the union results initially in a mass of undifferentiated cells. At a very early stage of foetal life the genetic blueprint determines the future physical characteristics of the child. To a large extent, people are programmed for death at the moment of conception, because of their genetic constitution.[1]

The physical differences between women and men are well known. They are different in physique, sexual organs, hormonal output, secondary sexual characteristics, and biological function. These differences result in different morbidity from sex-linked diseases, like haemophilia, and from some hormonally determined diseases. For instance, until the menopause women are protected by their female hormones from some diseases, like coronary thrombosis, which can kill men in early middle age. After the menopause, this protection no longer exists. There is some evidence that longevity is sex-linked.

Intelligence tests have shown a wide spectrum of individual aptitudes. There are measurable differences between women and men which are of statistical significance. Among the primary aptitudes, women excel in perceptual speed, verbal ability and colour sense. Girls talk earlier than boys and handle words better throughout life. Their superior verbal ability probably accounts for their apparent advantage over boys in being able to remember intelligible material. There is no real difference in rote memory when nonsense material is used in the testing. Men excel in spatial and number ability. The results of intelligence tests show that, when allowance is made for verbal and spatial ability differences, neither sex is superior to the other in overall ability. They also show that there is a wide range of individual ability so that some girls are good mathematicians, and some boys are good linguists. It is never possible to make statements like 'All girls are good at languages', nor 'All boys are good at science'.

Tests for fundamental differences between the personality traits of women and men are notoriously difficult to devise, because it is so hard to eliminate the influence of role stereotyping and social conditioning from the tests. Until recently, for instance, aggression was thought to be a character trait which was tied to genes and hormones. Women were thought to be less aggressive than men. Within the past two decades these assumptions have been challenged by a number of researchers. In a paper entitled 'Women and Work – Sex Differences and Society', prepared for the Department of Employment in Britain in 1974, Dr J. S. King reviewed some of the research into aggression and anxiety. He concluded :

The research studies outlined above seem to suggest that there are no differences in the amount of hostility felt by men and women, but rather differences in its mode of expression. Bennett and Cohen (1959), examining the personality patterns and contrasts of men and women, reported that women showed more anxiety about aggression than men, and greater controlled hostility. Although women tend to show less overt aggression, they reveal more hidden hostility. These findings suggest that women are at least as aggressive as men, but society forces them to control or channel this aggression and the consequence of this is an increase in apprehension and anxiety concerning aggression.[2]

Dr King also concluded that men tended to be just as anxious as women, but that they were more reluctant to admit it.

I would agree with this assessment for as I have already indicated, I do not think that aggression and anxiety, or any other personality trait, are sex-linked as such : in other words, I would not agree that aggression is a 'masculine' characteristic, nor that anxiety is a 'feminine' tendency. The question remains as to whether the fact that women and men express their anxiety in different ways is due only to cultural role conditioning, or whether the difference is the result of their biological sex, their femaleness or maleness.

Dr King's assessment of the strength of cultural role conditioning would seem to be supported by the work of some social anthropologists and ethologists who have shown that in some cultures women are trained to be aggressive hunters, and the men are trained to be gentle child minders.

It is tempting to think that the differences between women and men could be due to cultural conditioning and nothing else, and that if all children were reared as individuals, without sexist conditioning, they would all have the opportunity to become well integrated human beings who differed from each other only in biological function. This might conceivably happen if the world were to start again with a different set of women and men. There is no way of knowing. The world, however, is not in that hypothetical situation. Human beings who are alive today are what they are because of a long process of evolution. Such a long period of sexist conditioning may have resulted in the selective inbreeding of quantifiable differences between women and men. In any case, people who have tried to rear their children without sexist role conditioning and countries, like the Communist ones, which have written sexism out of their regimes, know that the effects of generations of sexist conditioning cannot be removed in a single generation, nor even in two or three generations. People have to live with the world as they find it in their own lifetimes, and all that they can do is to work towards a more just future for their grandchildren and great-grandchildren. Their willingness to do this is the measure of their commitment to their faith in the future.

To return to the question of measurable differences between women and men, there can be no doubt that, at the present time, they do exist.

It is probably impossible, at this period of history, to disentangle the differences which are due to genetic and hormonal factors from those which are due to biological and environmental needs. If the so-called 'feminine' and 'masculine' sex-linked concepts about personality differences are excluded from consideration, then there still remain some differences between women and men which are due to their femaleness and maleness. These differences make for the 'otherness' of women and men, but they also form the grounds of their 'togetherness'.

It is difficult to discuss femaleness and maleness in general terms, because the genetic sex and sexual orientation of individual human beings vary so greatly. It is, for instance, known that, since all human beings develop their sex organs from a rudimentary sex gland which has bipolar potential, women contain within their bodies elements of the male organs, and men contain vestigial female organs. It is also known that there is a wide range of genetic variation, so that some people can be born with the appearance of females when they are genetic males, and the reverse situation can also happen. Gender – a person's perception of his own sexual character – and anatomical sex need not correspond with each other, and as people grow into adult life they discover that they can be different from each other in sexual orientation, some being homosexual, others bisexual, transsexual, or heterosexual. The reproductive needs of the human race require that a high proportion of women and men should be sufficiently different from each other and heterosexually orientated so that they can breed children. If there are real differences in the way that femaleness and maleness affect the general attitudes and characters of women and men, it seems likely that those differences will be most obvious at the points where women and men are most different, yet most alike, that is in those areas of life which are directly related to their procreative and parental functions.

It often seems to me that the sexist view of the roles of women and men is based upon the supposition that because, in procreation, the vagina embraces the penis, women and men are like the 'female' and 'male' part of an electric plug which must exactly fit together to make an electrical connection. This view is expressed in the following quotation :

The male image is characterised by both men and women as strong, large, heavy. The female image is characterised as small, weak, soft, light : it is also dull, peaceful, relaxed, rounded, passive and slow. In short, women are perceived as the opposite of men.[3]

The same kind of idea about women and men being the opposite of each other is expressed by the sexual imagery which is used in everyday language : women are idealised when they are passive, submissive and receptive, and men are expected to be active, dominant and thrusting. When I think of the reality of sexual relationships, and their diversity, and when I carry the thought beyond sexual intercourse to the whole area of childbirth and child rearing, I cannot imagine that women and men correspond to the fantasy of being opposites to each other. Instead, I see them as complementary.

When I use the word 'complementary' I am using it to describe a relation between two objects which are not necessarily mirror images of each other, not exact opposites, but rather a relation in which two objects are indispensable to each other if there is to be a whole. For example, wax and wick are indispensable to each other if a candle is to burn. Women and men need each other if children are to be born. Wax and wick differ from each other, and can exist without each other, just as women and men are self-sufficient and can exist on their own. The analogy is not precise, of course, since a candle is not a living creature, and wax and wick are more different in kind from each other than women and men are, but the analogy serves to illustrate the meaning of the word.

It is in the context of that word 'complementary' that I set the relation of femaleness to maleness. It is in that context that I would say that women had a nurturing role and men a supportive one, although neither quality was the exclusive property of one sex.

Truth does not lie wholly in facts. In listing some of the factual differences between women and men, there is a danger of losing sight of some of the mystery of individuality and of the relationship between individuals. This mystery is expressed in an essay by François Chirpaz, entitled *The Difficult Experience of Difference* :

> The other is different because he is not I. He is in fact other than I – another : there is a gap between him and me. But the I is different from the other. I am not that other. I am different from him and different for him. The I is therefore constrained to recognise and accept this gap which it suddenly discovers and which keeps it at a distance from the other. I am not someone else and they are not me : we live at a certain distance, and the very distance is precisely what constitutes each of us in relation to the other.[4]

E

When people begin to understand the difference between sexist attitudes, which label particular human characteristics as 'feminine' or 'masculine', and non-sexist attitudes, which allow a proper distinction between women and men because they are female or male, they begin to be able to see each other in the light of their common humanity. They become aware that they have too much in common to denigrate and distrust each other, or to subordinate one another. In time that awareness grows into a desire for a real relationship of mutuality. People become aware that they do not need to remain imprisoned in the evils of sexism : and that is the beginning of their liberation.

5 Creative conflict

*'Pain without hope becomes hate; pain rooted in hope
becomes liberating and a liberator.'*
(Beatriz Melano Conch, Theologian, Argentina)

Few people become aware of themselves overnight. The discovery of
their identity as women or men takes place over a long period of time,
through the experience of their own inner world and through their
relations with other people. The awareness that they are not free to be
themselves, because they are prisoners of their own conditioning and of
other people's expectations of them, comes even more slowly to most
women and men.

In her book *The Feminine Mystique* Betty Friedan described how
one woman had realised how imprisoned she had been by her own idea
of what she should be like :

> I always knew as a child that I was going to grow up and go to
> college and then get married and that's as far as a girl has to think.
> After that your husband determines and fills your life. It wasn't till
> I got so lonely as the doctor's wife that I realised that I had to make
> my own life. I still had to decide what I wanted to be. I hadn't
> finished evolving at all. But it took me ten years to think it through.[1]

Betty Friedan discovered the same kind of uneasiness in many women
besides this doctor's wife. When she described 'the problem that has no
name', thousands of other women realised that she was talking about
a problem that afflicted their own lives. That corporate awareness grew
into a resurgence of active feminism in Western society.

For many years, the 'feminine mystique' had made women feel that
they ought to conform to the image they had of themselves as good
wives and mothers. Women did not suffer from great economic hardship in their middle-class, affluent, Western society, where this active

resurgence of feminism first took root. Life was not at all unpleasant for most women. This is how an American woman described her own life towards the end of the 1950s.

> I get up at six. I get my son dressed and then give him breakfast. After that I wash the dishes, and bathe and feed the baby. Then I get lunch and while the children nap, I sew or mend or iron and do all the other things I can't get done before noon. Then I cook supper for the family and my husband watches TV while I do the dishes. After I get the children to bed, I set my hair and then I go to bed.[2]

At the time she wrote this, this woman was living her life in a traditional middle-class style. In 1975 some women in Western society still enjoy that kind of life. There are many more women who have to combine that kind of routine at home with a part-time job in the community. Comparatively few wives and mothers pursue full-time careers outside their homes throughout their working lives. Single women usually have to be self-supporting.

Society today is different from that of the 1950s. It is, for instance, much more fluid than it used to be. There has been a growth of individualism. Alternative life styles flourish. In addition, the development of the communications industries over the last few years has made the world seem a much smaller place than it was before. Western people of today can see for themselves how women and men live with each other in the Second- and Third-World countries. Nothing can happen in the modern world without having some effect upon people's lives within a relatively short space of time.

Between 1960 and 1975 there was a resurgence of active feminism in Western society. This took many forms and provoked many conflict situations in indivuals, between people of different dispositions, and in society as a whole. Some of the results of these conflicts were destructive and many people remain bewildered as to the meaning of the eruption of women into social consciousness. The conflicts are continuing to have their effects upon the shape of society. The purpose of this chapter is to see how the conflict arising out of the feminist movement can become a creative preparation for the future liberation of women and men alike.

The purpose of conflict

Conflict happens whenever two or more objects, people or principles collide with each other. When such a collision takes place, either one or both sides must give way in favour of the other, or the two sides must remain locked in conflict. Many people fear conflict and take evasive action the moment they see the possibility ahead of them. Sometimes this decision is wise, but if a habit of avoiding conflict at any cost develops, then human beings rarely grow to their full potential. They have to change course so many times to avoid conflict that they become chameleon-like people without any identity of their own. On the other hand, there are some people who rush into conflict without thinking of the consequences at all. They enjoy the battle, but they risk overriding the opposition without caring that their opponents are getting hurt in the process. Alternatively, they find that they are not as strong as they thought they were, so they crumple when they come up against strong opposition, and get badly hurt themselves.

Those people who accept the necessity of some conflict in life know that the real purpose of conflict is not to win the battle, but to learn from the experience in such a way that it is possible to grow as persons. I believe that conflicts which arise as the result of sexism can provide people with opportunities to learn to become more whole, more fully human, more free to be themselves.

I cannot hope to cover many aspects of human conflict in a short space, so in this chapter I am going to consider only those conflicts which occur when women become aware that they are oppressed by sexist attitudes, actions and structures. I have chosen to look at the subject from a woman's point of view, because it is my experience that, at this point in time, women are more aware of their own than men's imprisonment.

Conflicts in women who become aware of their oppression

Some women never experience any conflict over their womanhood. They are those who have identified themselves wholly with their roles in life, either because their 'selves' are in harmony with their roles, or because they have successfully buried their 'selfish' needs below the surface of consciousness.

Many women, however, do become aware that they exist as people in their own right, with 'selfish' needs, as well as being women who are used to taking their identities from their roles as daughters, sisters, aunts, wives or mothers. When women do become aware that their real 'selves' are imprisoned in their roles, they can find themselves in a real tug-of-war conflict between what they know they want to be and do, and what they feel they ought to be and do. They are so accustomed to being dutiful women that they feel guilty at their desire to please themselves. They may feel even worse if they actually carry out their desires. On the other hand, women who habitually thwart their own needs may find that their frustration erupts into anger, which again induces guilt. Some unfortunate women are caught by their guilty feelings whichever way they decide to act.

Guilt is a very unpleasant emotion. Most people try to avoid it. Women who become guiltily aware of their own needs as human beings can deal with their feelings of guilt in several ways. Some women suppress their 'selfish' urges at once. They concentrate on encouraging the expression of 'unselfish' traits in themselves, which they know to be acceptable, and which conform to their own and other people's expectations of themselves. Some women turn their frustrated anger inwards on themselves in punishment for their disloyalty to their adopted roles. They become depressed and so assuage their guilt by suffering. Other women counter-attack their guilt by doing precisely what they want to do, without reference to their consciences, and in time they may succeed in forgetting their guilt; they may even learn to ignore their consciences. There are women who are fortunate enough to be able to share their feelings of conflict and guilt with others. They can find great relief from the experience, especially if their admissions are not greeted as if they were either dreadful sins, or peccadillos too trivial to be worthy of mention. These kinds of inner tension are often experienced by women who are trying to decide whether or not to return to outside work after a long spell at home as wives and mothers.

Women who become aware that they have subordinated their own needs as human beings to the demands of sexist-imposed 'feminine' roles have to learn to recognise the cause of their guilty feelings if they are to be able to use them creatively. They have to find the courage to stay with their guilt, and also with their sense of bewilderment about the meaning and importance of their experiences of conflicting desires. As they do this, they often find that they are able to overcome some of their fears and feelings of guilt so that they can step outside their familiar roles, and begin to test out the reality of their half-discovered 'selves'. In this they externalise their conflicts, and begin to meet opposition from others.

Conflicts between women and other people

Some people take the step towards conflict with others deliberately, in full knowledge of what will happen to them. Others, like myself, fall into external conflict almost by accident. Twelve years ago, I was scarcely aware that sexism existed. I had vaguely noticed it at medical school, but it had never seriously interfered with my own life, and I was working in a job I enjoyed. I was married, and pregnant with my fourth child. One day, I noticed a small item in a newspaper which reported the speech of a priest who had said that the sight of a pregnant woman in the sanctuary of a church would be indecent, and a blasphemy against God. I looked at my swelling body, for which I daily thanked God, and asked one question : 'Why?' It had never entered my mind that pregnancy was anything but beautiful and sacred, nor had it occurred to me that there was anything indecent about a pregnant woman working as a minister of a church in the sanctuary.

This one small cutting from a newspaper, coming at that particular time of my life, opened my eyes to my own blindness, and made me aware of the consequences of sexism. This experience sensitised me to the experiences of other women so that I began to notice how women were treated in society as well as in the Church, of which I was a member. I began to ask questions as to why women were treated as second-class citizens in all sections of society. I began with quite sensible enquiries like 'Why are things like this?' or 'Why can't a woman do this particular job?' Some of the answers were unsatisfactory and even the kindest tended to be evasive. Sometimes people replied, 'Because it has always been that way', or 'We know what is best for women', or even, 'Surely, you can be content with being a mother, can't you?' As I continued to ask questions, I began to encounter real hostility.

Hostility over sexist issues often comes from those sections of the community where people feel insecure in their sexual identities. For instance, it comes from men who feel threatened because they dare not admit to their conscious minds any hint of 'femininity' in themselves. It comes from 'superior' men with inferiority complexes, who have identified 'superiority' with 'masculinity'. It comes from some women who have repressed important parts of their personalities, and have submerged themselves in their 'feminine' roles. Both the insecurity and the repression are unconscious and beyond the control of their victims. The awkward question or the unusual behaviour of a woman provokes in the person questioned a feeling of anxiety which may turn to hostility. The person who is feeling hostile searches for a reason for this inexplicable feeling of antagonism towards a fellow human being, and produces an argument which satisfies the respondent even if it does not convince the questioner. The questioner often feels irritated at the answer given. Initially, at any rate, the questioner is probably just as insecure as the respondent, and so the conflict is inevitable, and at times very sterile.

A different kind of opposition, which is less easy to understand, comes from people whose minds are fixed in a pre-set pattern. These people do not appear to be hostile. They could not be described as woman-haters. Some of them are convinced that women are inferior to men. Others are certain that women have an important biological role to fulfil which must take precedence over all other considerations. In the eyes of people who think in this way, women's 'femininity' excludes them from participation in any decision-making processes outside the home, and also unfits them for positions of responsible authority. The pre-set attitudes are so strong that they embrace even single and childless women, so that they too find themselves excluded from full participation in the affairs of men. People who think in this pre-set way have pre-judged women as though they all fitted neatly into one or more role stereotypes.

Prejudices are acquired emotional attitudes which have been formed over a long period, so that they have become an intimate and fixed part of a person's character. Many prejudices are harmless enough. People all have their foibles, their likes and dislikes. Prejudices become more compelling when a large group of people is infected with the same attitude. For instance, there was a television programme in Britain about school children's attitudes towards racial prejudice. One young boy displayed very hostile feelings towards all his negro classmates. In a subsequent interview, this boy's father showed the same attitudes, and it became obvious that the father had learned his attitudes from his own parents, and had passed them on to his son without ever questioning their rightness. Prejudices like these cannot be thought of as harmless foibles, for they adversely affect so many relationships. They reinforce other people's prejudices, and even acquire respectability if they succeed in becoming incorporated into the prevailing culture which they infect. Differences in people's skin colour and sex are so obvious that they easily attract attention, which may be one reason why racist and sexist prejudices seem to be particularly widespread and deep-rooted.

Prejudices are often defended by irrational arguments. People, for instance, who dislike the thought of women being employed as bus drivers, will sometimes insist that women are unsuitable because *all* women are bad car drivers. When challenged to produce their evidence, they cite one instance of bad driving which they personally experienced or heard about some time before. Even when it is pointed out that one instance is one instance, and no more, such people often continue to assert their belief that *all* women are bad drivers, and unfit to be in charge of passengers. Their arguments may seem illogical to an unprejudiced person, but not to a prejudiced one. Such prejudices can be dangerous for they can be projected into expectations, where they can sometimes operate with precision. A prejudiced back-seat driver, for instance, can treat an unfortunate woman driver with such suspicion and fear that she is provoked into making a mistake. In this way the prejudice is reinforced.

It is often thought that hostility towards women, and prejudice against them, must yield to reason. In these deep-rooted and emotive situations, however, appeals to reason are not always helpful. Insecure or prejudiced people tend to defend their attitudes with complex rationalisations, so that the underlying causes of their original fear, bad experience or prejudice can remain hidden and unprobed; open challenge may cause the defendants to close their minds against women, and reinforce hostility and prejudice.

Women who find themselves in conflict with other people over sexist issues have to find creative ways of using the conflicts. There are several ways of doing this, and a good way of starting is to begin with their own prejudices so far as they are able, by staying with their own sense of insecurity, and their own hostile feelings, until they uncover their cause, or until they are overcome by common sense and patience.

Women can also use the pain of their own oppression to show them the problems which face those who have to endure other forms of oppression. Some time ago, I heard about the work of a white South African who works with negro women for their country's liberation from racism. On one occasion she had spent a weekend in conference.

There she had met a young Zulu woman who was about to emigrate, and they had spent some time together discussing their futures. Later, the white woman wrote about their meeting :

> At the end of the conference I looked for Mary and found her weeping. 'How can I leave my people, never to return?' she sobbed. She apologised for her emotions : 'A Zulu never cries,' she said.
>
> But those tears helped in some way to wash away a small part of the great wall of non-communication which has been created by prejudice and legislation. As two women, one black, one white, found in this experience that they trusted each other and cared enough to share the sorrow and the fears for the future, a new understanding came to each one. Gone were the protective façades of indifference; here were two human beings being human and exposing their humanity to each other.[3]

Many women have found that the size of other people's problems diminishes the importance of their own. They find great satisfaction in trying to help other people, even if they can do little or nothing about their own situation.

So often prejudices go underground. They are not openly voiced, but find expression in gossip, amusing jokes and secret votes against their victims. One of the most creative ways of using conflict is to encourage prejudiced people to speak their feelings aloud in the presence of their victims. Encounter of this sort gives the people involved a chance of seeing each other as fellow human beings. Women who are the victims of the prejudice can at least try to listen to the other person's admission of their feelings with understanding. Actual encounter with other people is a good antidote to fantasies about them. Male chauvinists often talk as if *all* women wanted to forsake their homes, husbands and families to pursue ambitious careers. Female chauvinists talk as if *all* women ought to put their small babies into 24-hour nurseries, while they go off and contribute their skills to society. While people have no contact with each other they can continue to believe their own half-true fantasies about one another. When, however, people can be brought into real contact with each other, they have some chance of getting to know one another as human beings, and a lot of the misunderstandings can evaporate.

Women who find that they are the victims of sexist prejudices have to learn, individually and corporately, to outlive the lies and half-truths which are told about them. One common prejudice against women focuses on their hormones:

> Physical factors, particularly the menstrual cycle and menopause, disqualify women from key executive jobs. If you had an investment in a bank, you wouldn't want the president of your bank making a loan under these raging hormonal influences at that particular period. (Edgar Bergman)[4]

One possible way of dealing with that kind of imputation is for women bankers to back their own judgements at times when they are premenstrual, and prove their competence; another way is to plan ahead so that they do not have to take important decision at times when they feel less able to make competent judgements. I certainly would not want my male bank manager to be under the influence of alcohol, or having a raging sexual fantasy, at the time he made an important decision. Although I know that some bank managers do drink a lot of alcohol and that some men do have violent sexual fantasies at inconvenient times, which are liable to distract their attention from mathematical figures, I do not assume that all bank managers are untrustworthy, without waiting for the proof. There is no need to assume that bank managers of either sex will be incompetent: all deserve the chance to be treated as inviduals. Here is another half-truth:

> When women are encouraged to be competitive too many of them become disagreeable. (Dr Benjamin Spock)

Men are rather unpleasant, too, when they are fighting for survival in a harsh world. The only creative thing to do with this remark is to find ways in which society can become less competitive and more caring.

I do not pretend that conflict is always creative. Women who become aware of being oppressed can become bitter. Their characters can become twisted by hatred if they fail to achieve their goals. They can find subtle ways of punishing other women and men for opposing them. They can learn to use what power they have destructively so as to treat men as men have treated them. I regard these side effects of conflict as inevitable risks which women have to take if they dare to allow themselves to get into conflict situations at all.

Women in sexist conflict situations need to use them as opportunities to find solidarity with each other in sisterhood, the kind of relation which enables women to discover their mutuality, and to unite in a common endeavour.

Conflicts between women and sexist structures

Individual women can do very little by themselves against sexist structures. If they try, the conflict is likely to be very one-sided, and the individual finds herself banging her head against a brick wall, if indeed she can find the brick wall at all. Sexism is difficult to recognise because it hides behind so many assumptions, customs and laws that people have always taken for granted. In Western society, at any rate, the individual person has little hope of penetrating the complexities of the tax laws, social security regulations and civil laws which hide the wall from sight. Individuals quickly discover that if they are to achieve any success at all against sexist structures, they have to unite with each other and draw on their reserves of expertise to reach the fabric of the resistant structure.

Formerly, when women tried to unite, they did so in the face of considerable difficulties, as Simone de Beauvoir has pointed out :

> The women's effort has never been anything more than a symbolic agitation. They have gained only what men have been willing to grant; they have taken nothing, they have only received.
>
> The reason for this is that women lack concrete means for organising themselves into a unit which can stand face to face with the correlative unit. They have no past, no history, no religion of their own.[6]

Since Simone de Beauvoir wrote that in 1949, women have been gathering themselves together, to discover their past, to celebrate their achievements, to develop their own identities and to formulate their own ideologies. Women have not yet formed themselves into the kind of correlative units which could act as a revolutionary force in society. They have not yet decided whether they want to form such a power-based unit, or whether there are more creative alternatives to pursue for the betterment of the whole of society. Meantime, women are gaining experience and are tasting success in a number of different fields.

Some of their success is coming about through the conversion of men to their way of thought. The union of women and men in partnership with each other, so as to apply economic, social and political pressures to bear on sexist structures, is one of the most creative practical steps towards their mutual liberation, but it is a step which cannot be taken without a good deal of preparation independently of each other. Part of this preparation will be the acknowledgement that there is a price to pay for freedom. At the Berlin 'Consultation on Sexism', we were told :

> I don't know what you have to pay. Maybe, it means for you to be different and not understood by people who are important to you. To cut yourselves off from traditions and habits you have grown up with. To keep a sense of suffering alive in yourselves and others in order not to get used to the lack of freedom. To abandon any absolute certainty about the 'right way'. We could think of many more ways of paying for liberation : fear, insecurity, pain, bad conscience, despair, being 'outcast'.[7]

This statement is not rhetoric; it is based upon hard facts. In California, for instance, the State Department of Health commissioned a report about the causes of the steep rise in the suicide rate of women in recent years. This investigation was carried out by Mrs Nancy Allen, who said in her report :

> The rise in the suicide rate is part of the price women have to pay for their liberation. Women lack the experience, the training to cope with the risks, the performance stress, the conflicts and the defeats of their work. A woman cannot yet accept failure in her profession and accept, understand and come to terms with the personal, financial and professional consequences without suffering depression, or even resorting to suicide.[8]

The price of conflict is paid, not only by women who are oppressed by sexism, but also by the men who symbolise oppression. These men become the victims of a process not of their own making, for sexism is a way of life they have inherited. Some men feel very much threatened when women ask questions, challenging their attitudes. Others suffer broken marriages as a result of the liberation upheaval. Some men lose their self-confidence and even become impotent when women take the initiative and demand equality in sexual intercourse. An equally painful price is paid by women who have colluded with men in upholding sexist attitudes and structures. They too find themselves threatened, and are very often upset by sexist conflict.

Suffering is a price people must pay in pursuing their goals. There are many different paths towards the goal of freedom. Along the way some dream dreams, some fight, some pray, some think it right to resist oppression and some think it right to restrain growth. Some find that 'pain rooted in hope becomes a liberator', if they allow that pain to take root in their lives.

Personally, I have learnt that I can oppose only those whom I have first learnt to love. I would like to pass on one affirmation which has stood me in good stead in the heat of conflict when I have been opposed with great hatred. The words have burnt themselves into my life as a kind of prayer which I use to remind myself of the humanity of those who are sexists :

I will call you brother, even though you will not call me sister.
I will reach out to you, even though you will not reach out to me.
I will affirm our mutuality as persons seeking to make a common
    witness, even though you are not free to do so. [9]

6   The beginning of freedom

'Better to die on one's feet than to live on one's knees.'
(Camus, *The Rebel*)

When the victims of sexism have become aware of their oppression and their own humanity, they discover their need for the freedom to become fully themselves. As they encounter the conflicts which are the consequences of the liberation struggle, they often find that they experience sudden and deep fear. The price to be paid for even partial freedom from sexism seems inordinately high. People who have struggled towards freedom may have seen marriages break up. Women may have lost their jobs because of their reputations as 'trouble-makers'. They may have found out that, although they have been able to survive the inevitable back-lash of hostility, they have had to watch other people go to the wall. They have seen women with good chances of success in business or a profession; and later heard that they had thrown their chances away. They have seen disillusioned liberationists give up the struggle and settle for a life of boredom. They have even seen former allies become indifferent, and they may have known women who have become successful, but have done nothing to help their sisters. People who reach this stage find that they are tired of the struggle and are fearful of what the future may hold.

This is a terrifying stage in the liberation struggle. It is a common experience in any struggle which involves progress from slavery to freedom. At the beginning, slaves are conscious most of all of their shackles, which chafe them and prevent them from doing what they feel they might want to do. They have only the vaguest idea of what freedom might entail. As the chains are loosened, either through their own efforts or through the compassion of other people, they begin to notice the chains less, and to think more about what it might be like to be permanently free. Suddenly, the security of their chains seems preferable to the unknown responsibility of freedom. Moreover, they cannot see how they will use their freedom when they get it. Women who find themselves at this stage of life are afraid of how they will become independent, find their own jobs, get on without the help of a man telling them what to do, and how they will manage without the privileges which they enjoyed because of their sex, privileges like being cosseted, flattered and flirted with. Men worry about how they will get on without their role of domination and authority, and their stereotyped roles as door openers, escorts, providers and seducers. Their doubts are reinforced by some popular misconceptions about what liberation really means.

Liberation is one of those words whose meaning has been twisted through misuse. Its literal meaning is release, and the word poses two questions by implication : one is release from what, and other release for what. In popular use in Western society, liberation has become a synonym for selfish freedom. It has come to mean being free from all responsibility so that people can do as they please, where they please, whatever they want to do and whenever they want to do it. This seems a very limited and pointless concept of liberation. There would be little point in people gaining their freedom from oppression if all that meant was that they would have no purpose in their lives, no responsibilities towards other people or the community as a whole. Few people would think it worth fighting for the freedom to be alone, serving no one but themselves. There may be some people who are willing to purchase their own freedom at the expense of other people's lives, liberties and happiness, but ultimately they find that the end result of total commitment to that kind of action is to become unloving and unloved, and they live their lives in a kind of hell which is of their own making. True liberation cannot be thought of in those terms at all. The majority of people who participate in liberation struggles are asking to be freed from all sorts of oppressions. Some of these come from inside a person's own personality : jealousy, for instance, can be a tyrannical master from which a person seeks deliverance in order to be able to love truly and freely. Other oppressions, like sexism, come from outside a person, so that people seek to be freed from evils such as poverty, hunger, disease, injustice, enslavement to fear, or the tyranny of subservience. People usually seek liberation in order to be free to have and do things which they consider to be good : they want to be happy, healthy people, for instance, or to be free to use their talents in the service of the community and to receive reasonable rewards. In the context of sexism the ultimate goal of liberation is partnership between free people. I know of no better definition of partnership than the one which was hammered out in the discussions at the conference in Berlin :

> Partnership is a voluntary unit formed between two or more people acting from a common base of respect and trust, recognising each other's rights and conscious of each other's differences, sacrificing equally, and working together within a pattern they set for them-selves, towards a common goal, each contributing to the best of her or his abilities to achieve what no one of them could have achieved alone.[1]

Even when people have properly understood what liberation from sexism is about, and have seen to what use they might put their freedom, they are often still afraid because they see that what began as a bid for freedom has suddenly involved them in a revolution, and they are not at all sure that that is what they bargained for in the first place, or really want for the future.

I must make it clear that when I use the term 'revolution' I am not referring to the violent overthrow of one unjust system by another equally oppressive system, but am using it in the way in which Jurgen Moltmann defined it :

> I understand revolution to mean a transformation in the founda-tions of a system, whether of economics, of politics, of morality, or of religion. All other changes amount to evolution or reform.[2]

I think that when people realise that liberation from sexism means that the foundations of patriarchal society will be transformed and replaced by new foundations, they understand that the women's movement is a revolutionary one. If even those who are protagonists of liberation from sexism are afraid of the implications of revolution, then their opponents may be even more afraid. This is one of the major reasons why the women's movement is so widely resisted, especially in those institutions which are hierarchical and male dominated, like various religious bodies. In this context, it is becoming apparent that some religious members of the women's movement are as radical as those outside religious institutions. Mary Daly, a radical American theologian has expressed this in connection with the Christian Church :

> It cannot be stressed too strongly that the system and the entire

F

conceptual apparatus of Christian theology, developed under the conditions of patriarchy, have been the products of males and that in large measure these serve the interests of sexist society. Given these conditions it is not surprising that women who are attempting to challenge the structures, symbols, and values of Christianity are at times not radical and daring enough, stopping at the goal of mere reforming within pre-established social structures and/or semantic structures that reflect the latter. To get beyond this requires a resurrection experience – beginning to hear and to speak new words. This means real cerebral work, but the work ahead is hardly a merely cerebral exercise. It is growing that has to go on – a growing that takes place on the boundary of patriarchal institutions and their legitimations.[3]

Mary Daly is not alone. A similar point was made by another woman, writing in an English Roman Catholic journal :

> If we do nothing and only talk of the revolution we shall never get there, but if we make the means into ends themselves we shall not necessarily get there either. Previous femininist campaigns which allowed themselves to be content with the achievements of their nearest aims (for instance, the vote) are responsible to a considerable degree for the slow progress and present difficulty experienced by the movement for women's liberation.[4]

Rightly, women's liberation is considered to be a wider and more revolutionary concept than that of equal opportunities for women or 'women's rights'. It is interesting that in England some members of the Anglican Church view the move towards the ordination of women to the priesthood as an attempt by the women's liberation movement to overturn the established structure of the ordained ministry. That could be a misconception of the issue about ordination. Supporters of women's ordination might have theological reasons for their desire, or even possibly desire equal opportunities for women to share in the hierarchical structure. Liberationists, however, might see ordination only as a step towards the transformation of the Church so that it might become a community of women and men who were altogether free from hierarchical domination by a priestly caste. Some liberationists might even see the ordination of women as a retrogressive step, and therefore bypass the issue altogether.

If then, people have cause to be afraid of transformation, it has to be asked whether it is the transformation itself of which people are so afraid, or the means by which this will be accomplished. I think that some of the deepest fears which people have about revolution concern the means by which it is to be achieved rather than the end itself, and it is because of anxiety over strategy that people become afraid of claiming their freedom.

In the matter of strategy to be employed in overcoming sexism, I do not believe that there is only one right strategy to use. Sexism is but one of a number of different oppressive evils which are being fought in the world, and it might be helpful to look at some of the strategies which have been used by others in liberation struggles. Two possible ways are shown by the lives of Martin Luther King and Camillo Torres, who both died because of their participation in the liberation struggles of their people.

In America, Martin Luther King thought it right to make non-violent protest the corner-stone of his campaign. He was a man who showed the world that he could fight evil acts and oppressive laws openly and persistently, while at the same time he treated the people who perpetrated the evil acts, and who upheld oppressive laws, with the respect due to them as human beings. King, an American negro and Baptist minister, totally identified himself with his own oppressed people in their struggle against racism. In the course of that struggle he opposed many white people who were oppressing black people, but he refused to be diverted into fighting white people simply because they were white-skinned. He knew that they needed to be freed from their enslavement to their roles as oppressors, and when they did find their freedom, many of them united with him in the struggle against racism. By his total response he not only stood on his own feet, but also enabled millions of other people to stand on theirs.

In South America, in very different circumstances, Camillo Torres was opposing political oppression, and saw no alternative but to use violence as a strategy. When he took the first steps towards his death, Torres said :

My analysis of Colombian society made me realise that revolution is necessary to feed the hungry, give drinks to the thirsty, clothe the naked and procure a life of well-being for the needy majority of our people. I believe that the revolutionary struggle is appropriate for the Christian and the priest. Only by revolution, by changing the concrete conditions of our country, can we enable men to practise love for each other.[5]

The non-violent protest that was appropriate to the American situation was inappropriate in the Colombian situation, as Torres saw it, so he used his Catholic priesthood in guerrilla warfare.

These two types of revolutionary strategy have already been used in the liberation struggles against sexism which have taken place on a world-wide scale. In the First World, women have been involved in the violent protest of the suffragette movement. They have also participated in non-violent protest, and have latterly benefited from a resurgence of feminist solidarity and symbolic and non-violent protest. The Second World prides itself that it has largely overcome sexism through social revolution, some of which has involved the use of violence. The Third World faces the oppressions of poverty and political power, and there the sexist struggle is considered to be a secondary issue. I have found that Third-World women, in particular, expect to gain their own liberation as part of the expected social revolution, and they do not discount the possibility of the use of violence.

It has been said, with some justification, that neither of these strategies is effective in the effort to release both women and men from their enslavement to sexism. Women make up over half the human race and have, therefore, been designated as members of the Fourth World, and the most oppressed section of the world-wide community. The problems of sexism are so universal and basic that the transformation of the relations between women and men will demand the united efforts of each in a peaceful revolution. Although this may seem a well-nigh impossible task at present, nevertheless, at the moment when people feel the most afraid they need to affirm their trust in each other and their hope for the future. This is well expressed by Moltmann :

> Hope must draw the hoped for future already into the misery of the present and use it in practical initiatives for overcoming this misery. Through criticism and protest on the one hand, and creative imagination and action on the other, we can avail ourselves of freedom for the future.[6]

Before they can seize the hope of which Jurgen Moltmann speaks, however, many people still have to face the other and less obvious fear that the transformation of the familiar patriarchal structure of society might result in a situation which would be worse than the one people at present know. They fear that order will be replaced by chaos. Since at this time in history, the world as a whole appears to be going through a transition period in which there are so many uncertainties about the future, it is not surprising that people should wish to cling to the familiar structures where they can, and for as long as they can. There can be no complete answer to this fear because no one does know what the future will be like when women and men join with each other in full partnership to work towards their joint future. This fear is counterbalanced, and often outweighed, by deep-rooted impulses which inspire human beings to want to explore the unknown. The fear of the unknown is overcome by those who can let go of the past for the sake of the future, and there is, fortunately, plenty of evidence that this is happening all over the world.

The quality of any revolution will be judged by the use people make of their freedom, once they have been liberated from oppression. When women and men find that they are free from the worst material and psychological restraints of sexism they are free to use their initiative in practical ways. Their activities are most fruitful when they can combine 'criticism and protest on the one hand, and creative imagination and action on the other' into one course of action which is creative rather than destructive. Women all over the world have been particularly quick to learn this lesson, and they are able to use their partial freedom to unite protest with action, in very concrete ways. Of course, women have always taken practical action to help themselves and each other, but now they are not so content to leave the structures of their communities unchanged : instead, they are taking action with the deliberate intention of changing the structures of the societies in which they live. In Berlin, I saw a liberation poster which said :

Sisterhood is blooming. Springtime will never be the same.

I could believe that by the time I had heard of some of the things which women were doing to help each other up and down the world :

In a Jamaican village, the women's custom was to wash by the river. This involved walking to the river, keeping the children home from school to carry the water. Together, the women established a centre where they could come and erected a wash house with complete facilities for laundry. They appointed a committee to organise the project; some were assigned to keep the children, some to look after the place. This project enabled them to make more money from their washing. The older children could go to school, and the babies were cared for at the place where their mothers worked.

In Papua, New Guinea, a group of Churchwomen in one village was trying to protect their property. They formed a Trade Union to check up on the things the merchant ordered. If he ordered something they didn't want, they boycotted him. This is the way they protected one another from being exploited into buying unnecessary objects and not having enough money for the necessities.

In Canada, Sioux Indians faced many difficulties. They were hopeless and angry. One group organised itself to make native handicrafts. The co-operative has become a major tourist attraction. This has not only given them money but pride in their abilities and joy in working together.

In the Caribbean area, a group of women who marketed fish had one group of fishermen who caught beautiful fish, but before they could get them to market the fish spoiled. So the women borrowed money from a development fund, bought a truck and ice, and furnished their own transportation. The business flourished, so that the fishermen were angry that they had not had the idea first.

In England, two Lesbian women found themselves misunderstood and socially isolated. They started a 'collective' for homosexual women, and have transformed the lives of many women. Their collective has done much to help people to understand homosexuality better.

In Japan, a woman called Suiko Shiga worked at the Tokyo machine industry, doing office work in a factory where most of the workers were men. The management and the men agreed that women workers should be required to retire at the age of thirty. As a result many women had to leave work. Suiko Shiga wrote a protest paper insisting on employment rights, and distributed it to the other workers at the factory gate. Having exposed the injustice, she gained enough support to regain her original job. Her anger and her success have been small but important steps towards smashing systematic injustice for the millions of working women in Japan.

In England, Erin Pizzy started to take 'battered wives' into an old empty house. Within weeks she was flooded with applications. She and some co-workers started the Chiswick Women's Aid Centre, raised some money, and persuaded the Government to give a financial grant towards the work.[7]

Other women are taking the same kinds of initiative over a variety of issues all over the world. They are gaining in confidence and developing new skills. They are becoming experts in their chosen fields of work. Some of them are taking their new freedoms for granted : others know that they will have to struggle for a long time before they know freedom at all. More and more women are using their freedom, partial though it may be, to help men to become free from their roles as the oppressors of women. I remember, for instance, meeting a priest whose paternal attitude had been oppressive to some women in his congregation. Eventually, one of the women had told him how his attitudes had prevented their growth as people. He took her comments seriously, although they had hurt him, and much later he told me that he had found the true authority of leadership only when he had learnt to share it with other people.

In recent years, men have increasingly used their own partial freedom to align themselves with women. They have combined protest with creative action in a variety of ways. I have, for instance, known a respected Member of Parliament to keep watch alongside women at an all-night vigil on behalf of the women's movement. I have seen men stand up to be counted, as Dr Charles Willie did when he preached the sermon at the controversial ordination of twelve American women in 1974. On that 'irregular' occasion he said :

I participate in this service today not because I wanted to speak out but because I could not remain silent. I speak neither as an officer of the Church nor as a professor of any school, but as a child of God who decided to make no peace with oppression. I stand ready to suffer the consequences of my action, knowing, as Martin Luther King said, that unearned suffering is redemptive.[8]

I have seen men suffer ridicule for their solidarity with women. I have known men speak out with prophetic vision, as Dr Philip Potter has done :

The liberation of women will mean the liberation of men. Booker T. Washington, the black American leader, once said : 'You can't keep a person in the gutter without remaining there.' The same can be said of sexism. Neither men nor women will become truly human unless this disease of sexism is diagnosed and cured.[9]

This growing awareness in men surely must be significant for the future relations between women and men, especially when they discover that they share the same ultimate goals.

This 'dark night' of fear and doubt which envelops individuals, and whole communities, should not be underestimated, for it is a potent enemy to human beings who undertake any journey from slavery towards freedom. Yet, on the journey from the slavery of sexism to the freedom of partnership there are these oases of experience. Sustained by hope and encouraged by success, women and men can begin to taste freedom. It is important to have these tastes, because in the liberation struggle there are long periods when people lose sight of the goal ahead. They need the good experiences to offset the bad times, and they need some kind of vision of what the future might be like, if they are not to get totally lost in the day-to-day encounters with sexism that are part of ordinary life. I cannot forget the haunting words which I once heard, in which the longing itself is the vision :

> I want a woman's revolution like a lover.
> I lust for it, I want so much this freedom,
> this end to struggle and fear and lies
> we all exhale, that I could die just
> with the passionate uttering of that desire.
> Just once, in this my only life time to dance
> all alone and bare on a high cliff under cypress trees
> with no fear of where I place my feet.
> To even glimpse what I might have been and never, never
> will become, had I not had to 'waste my life' fighting.
> for what my lack of freedom keeps me from glimpsing.[10]

7 The search for partnership

'And perhaps the sexes are more related than we think, and the great renewal of the world will perhaps consist in this, that man and maid, freed of all false feeling and reluctance, will seek each other, not as opposites, but as brother and sister, as neighbours, and will come together as human beings, in order simply, seriously and patiently to bear in common the difficult sex that has been laid upon them.' (R. M. Rilke, *Letters to a Young Poet*, 1906)

In May 1851 there was a Women's Rights Convention at Akron, Ohio. To that meeting came Sojurner Truth, a former slave. She was a tall, gaunt negro woman. One of her contemporaries said that she was wearing a grey dress and a white turban. The leaders of the movement were afraid when they saw her 'march deliberately into the church, walk with an air of a queen up the aisle and take her seat upon the pulpit steps'. There she sat, throughout the first day, listening to the speeches.

In those days, very few women dared to get to their feet to speak at a public meeting, so most of the speeches were by men who were hostile to thoughts of giving women any rights at all. Frances Gage, a contemporary of Sojurner Truth, was in the chair. She wrote an account of the meeting. She described the low morale of the women on the second day of the meeting when, as she put it, 'the august teachers of the people were seemingly getting the better of us'. The atmosphere was stormy.

Sojurner Truth got to her feet, and moved slowly and solemnly to the front of the assembly. There was a hissing sound of disapprobation from the audience. Frances Gage pleaded for a few minutes' silence to let the negro woman be heard. Later she wrote :

At her first word there was a profound hush. She spoke in deep tones which, though not loud, reached every ear in the house. 'That man over there says that women need to be helped into carriages, and lifted over ditches, and to have the best place everywhere.

Nobody helps me into carriages or over mud puddles, or gives me any best place.'

And raising herself to her full height, and her voice to a pitch like rolling thunder, she asked :

'And ain't I a woman? Look at me ! Look at my arm (and she bared her right arm to the shoulder showing her tremendous muscular power). I have ploughed and planted, and gathered into barns, and no man could head me ! And ain't I a woman? I could work as much and eat as much as a man – when I could get it ! And bear the lash as well ! And ain't I a woman? I have borne thirteen children and seen most of them sold into slavery, and when I cried out in my mother's grief none but Jesus heard me ! And ain't I a woman?

'Then they talk about this thing in the head; what do they call it? ['Intellect' whispered someone near.] That's it. What's that got to do with women's rights or negros' rights? If my cup won't hold but a pint, and yours holds a quart, wouldn't you be mean not to let me have my little half measure full?'

The cheering was loud and long. She continued : 'Then that little man in black, there, he says that women won't have as much rights as men, 'cause Christ wasn't a woman ! Where did your Christ come from? From God and a woman ! Man had nothing to do with him.'

Amid roars of applause she returned to her corner.[1]

In writing this account Frances Gage said that she had never before seen anything like the magical influence that Sojurner Truth exerted at that meeting. It turned the sneers and jeers of the excited crowd into notes of respect and admiration.

The search for true partnership between women and men cannot properly begin until people have risen off their knees to stand to their full height as human beings, as Sojurner Truth did. Human beings are individuals, and progress towards partnership varies greatly for different people and societies. Progress is more like the growth of children : it proceeds intermittently, and is sometimes negligible, sometimes considerable.

Among societies afflicted by sexism the struggle to become fully human has so far taken place mainly among women, for it is they who are most aware of their oppression. Men have only just begun to discover their own captivity to their roles as oppressors. As people become more free to be themselves, they grow more aware of other people and of their own potential for relationship.

This chapter is concerned with the way in which women and men can discover each other in a context of a common goal of mutual interdependence. It looks at ways in which women and men can co-operate with each other to make full use of the opportunities which already exist for partnership, so that in time they may discover new and better ways of living together.

Preparing for partnership

Before people can be successful at living with each other they have to learn to live with themselves, at least to the point where they have some insight into their personalities, and some self-control.

When people dislike certain things about themselves they tend to throw, or project, the disliked qualities into other people so that they can fight the 'bad' bits of themselves in others. One pre-condition for living in partnership is for individuals to be able to acknowledge some of their disliked characteristics so as to be able to integrate them into their conscious personalities. This is not as simple a task as it sounds, for people are adept at concealing from themselves what they really are, and what they are doing. Once, however, individuals have recognised parts of their own personalities of which they were formerly ashamed or even unaware, they are free to decide what to do with them. A housewife, for instance, who has formerly thought that ambition was 'unfeminine', to the point where she suppressed or even repressed it, can discover a new freedom once she has acknowledged its existence in herself. If she can accept ambition as part of herself, without threat to her womanhood, she can decide how she will use it. She might decide that, for her personal happiness, her ambition should be channelled into home or a non-competitive way of life. Alternatively, she could choose to try to realise her ambition, but control it so that it does not make her into a thoroughly unpleasant person, or she might even decide that being unpleasant was part of the price she had to pay for success. Self-understanding of this kind gives people a chance, even if they do not use it, to enjoy being themselves. The ability to enjoy being a human being is probably the most important pre-condition for any good working relationship between people.

In learning to enjoy their humanity people have to come to terms with their own particular sex and sexual identity. It is now known that it is impossible to divide the whole human race into people who can be classified into only two categories, females or males. There are only people, whose sex is an important feature of themselves, and individuals have to work out for themselves the relationship that their anatomical sex has to their sexual orientation and self-perception.

Many people who are active in liberation struggles are there, and have become what they are, because of their own struggles to reach a self-understanding and wholeness that has formerly escaped them. There is no shame in that. At the same time, it is important that people outside the immediate orbit of the struggle should realise that because some active protagonists of liberation seem to be 'disturbed' people, the justice of their cause is not invalidated by their 'disturbance'. It is equally important that people who know that part of their search for justice is an external projection of an internal struggle, should not stop working towards a more just external partnership between women and men in every section of society. They are the courageous ones, who have undertaken a task which many other people dare not do, and they are most likely to resolve both their internal tensions and the external injustices of sexism if they are willing to continue to search for freedom in themselves and in their external relationships.

The journey from the slavery of sexism to the freedom of partnership is a long one. The difficulties and hardships of the journey cannot be minimised, but they need not be magnified out of all proportion, for the search for true partnership is an exciting adventure as well as a tough assignment. On the journey there are companions, and there is a great deal that people can do to help each other along the way.

Learning to value each other

While women are struggling to find themselves, and men continue to be afraid of losing themselves, if they allow women to become their full partners, it may be inevitable that they should sometimes denigrate each other. Destructive criticism may relieve the critics' feelings and serve to unite them with one another, but it seldom helps them to see other people as they really are. When people are really trying to get together they look for and accept each other's strengths as well as their weaknesses. They can then begin to achieve what the poet Rilke was talking about when he spoke of women and men coming together 'as human beings, in order simply, seriously and patiently to bear in common the difficult sex that has been laid upon them'.

Historically, there have been some remarkable partnerships between women and men in which each partner has evoked the strengths of the other, so that together they have achieved more than they probably would have done on their own. Most of my own examples are drawn from the Christian tradition and my own culture, because I know these best, but they could be multiplied many times over in different cultures. The Church has been particularly rich in these partnerships. To name but a few, for example, there are St Francis and St Clare, St Francis de Sales and St Jeanne de Chantal, St Vincent de Paul and Louise de Marillac. All these men were quite unusual in their attitudes to their partners : for example, St Francis encouraged St Clare to run away from home to follow the Lady Poverty; St Francis de Sales did not stop St Jeanne de Chantal when she left her home and children to found the Visitation Order; St Vincent de Paul urged Louise de Marillac to take her nuns out into the streets and poor homes, at a time in history when the rules governing the behaviour of nuns dictated that they should say within convent walls. In fact, nearly every foundress of a women's religious order had the support of a strong-minded man behind her. It is true that the man was 'over' her, but in the letters which they wrote to each other it is possible to sense that their relations with each other were closer to partnership than was at all usual for their time. Outside the religious orders, there were other fruitful relationships between women and men : Sidney Herbert sustained Florence Nightingale : Elisabeth Garrett Anderson owed much to her father, Newsom, without whose support she would have been unable to become the first English woman to qualify as a doctor in her own country; her sister, Millicent, founded a society to work for women's suffrage by constitutional methods; a Roman Catholic scholar, Baron von Hügel, exerted a formative influence on the life of his Anglican pupil, Evelyn Underhill. Husbands, too, have been instrumental in supporting their wives : both Elisabeth and Millicent Garret found husbands who were in sympathy with their aims; Catherine Booth must have startled her husband when she asked him to let her 'say a word' from the pulpit, but he came down and let her go up to become a noted evangelist in her own right; Josephine Butler's husband wholeheartedly supported her fight to help women who were the victims of the double standard of morality which prevailed in their day.

Many women of today, including myself, testify to the help they have received from their husbands, and from other male colleagues who have helped them towards fuller lives by treating them as adults fit for partnership. The joys of these relationships outweigh the sufferings which can come to women through other people's antagonism. Women are also learning to value the work and lives of other women. The world owes a great deal to its women, though they are not given as much credit for their achievements as are the heroes of history. So much of women's work has gone unsung because it has been done behind the scenes and has been under the nominal supervision of male 'leadership'. When, for instance, one thinks of the thousands of women who have spent their lives away from their home countries as missionary teachers, nurses, doctors or evangelists it seem incredible that men should have taken the credit for so much of their work, and that so many Churches still refuse leadership positions to their women. When one thinks of the strength of women in adversity it seems strange that they should accept the idea that they were the 'weaker sex'. Fortunately, women are no longer forgotten. All over the world women are studying their own past inheritance, and are paying tribute to the work of other women as they learn to take greater pride in the achievements of their own sex.

Learning to value each other as members of one community, in which needs and tasks can be shared and receive proper recognition, is an important stage in people's experience of relationship, and enables them to take their full share in the responsibilities of joint partnership.

New dimensions of partnership

The marital relationship is one model of partnership between women and men. It is probable that much of the fear that surrounds the women's movement comes from the belief that marriage will be abolished after the revolution. This is a very deep fear present in both women and men, so much so that, for instance, the women gathered in Berlin for the 'Consultation on Sexism' avoided really creative discussion on possible alternatives to monogamous marriage, which is still the norm among Christians, although not, of course, among adherents of some other religions. Those who belong to liberation movements cannot avoid this issue. Revolution does mean transformation, and the structure of marriage is bound to be transformed from the common Western pattern of today, where the husband is considered to be the head of the family, the economic provider and the ultimate source of authority. Transformation does not necessarily mean abolition, but it does mean that there will have to be a radical reappraisal of the relationships of the members of the family to each other, and to people outside the immediate family.

The typical family in the West is self-contained. However they decide to live, one of the couple makes the task of caring for the children her or his priority. Mutual care of the home is usually only possible where there are no children, or the people concerned are rich enough or old enough to stay at home together. Within this overall pattern there is a wide range of variation among individual families. It is still difficult for families at either end of the range to adopt their chosen life styles without guilt. In Western society, families where the wife never works outside the home, are as guilt-laden as the families where wife and husband have reversed roles completely. Members of both groups can be heard making defensive statements on behalf of their way of life, although this guilt is slowly receding as people become more free from conventional behaviour.

The self-contained or 'nuclear' family is being challenged by a variety of alternative life styles, which all make use of an extended family system. Some people, Christians among them, are living in small communes. In some communes there are only married couples and the pair-bonding arrangement remains normative. Others include unmarried people as part of their extended family. Yet others have adopted communal marriage, so that partners are freely exchanged. There are also some celibate communes, notably in the Christian Church, where women and men share a household, but not their bodies, with each other. There are homosexual families, either of the nuclear type or of the communal type, some of which are sexually active and some celibate. There are some people who depend on others to be able to live as hermits.

It is noticeable that the larger communes need more rules to govern the behaviour of their members. Individuals have to adapt themselves to the requirements of the group, and deviations from the norms of behaviour for the group are not well tolerated. It is known, for instance, that in polygamous or polyandrous societies sexual deviations are infrequently overt, because deviant individuals are afraid to express themselves openly in such a close-knit society. Similarly, although homosexual and heterosexual people can live together in a celibate commune, such communes do not easily accept married couples into their midst, since the exceptions to the rule would make it difficult for the celibates to keep to their rule. On the other hand, small communes of like-minded people offer the kind of work-sharing opportunities to their individual members which lighten the burden of work for all. Such communes make full use of the various talents of their members. They also strengthen individuals in their resolve to stand out against the prevailing mores of society. This is probably why an increasing number of Christians are grouping themselves into small communes. By doing this they preserve their Christian life style as a group. Individual members of the commune are not so likely to lapse from the practice of Christianity as they are when they find themselves in isolation, living among non-Christians.

These alternative life styles may go some way towards helping people to overcome their sexist attitudes, but they do not necessarily do so, and it does not seem likely that by itself the abolition of nuclear marriage would stop sexism. I am not convinced that monogamy is as oppressive as some members of the women's movement feel it to be, nor am I convinced that the liberation of women necessarily involves the overthrow of monogamy and/or the nuclear family, as some Christians fear will happen, and as some liberationists hope will happen. I do, however, believe that marriages and marital relationships of all kinds will be transformed when people become free to discover new kinds of responsible relations with each other.

It does not seem likely that new kinds of partnerships between women and men can come about until women can learn to be more critical of the 'male' way of life, and until men can learn to see what is good in the 'female' way of life. Only in that way can women and men learn from each other what to discard and what to develop, so that together they can build a new future for themselves, in which the best of the old life styles could be gathered into the new lives which they freely choose for themselves.

The value of women and men to each other

Whenever the subject of parity between women and men comes up in conversation, it is commonly assumed that women want to share the responsiblilities and privileges of men, and be free to live as men now live in society. It is scarcely ever assumed that men would want to live as women now do. During my life as a doctor, I have listened to the life stories of a great many women and men. I have often wondered why men's lives were considered to be so desirable that women would want to emulate them. For example, I have known men worry about their potency as men. I have seen men driven by their own ambition. I have sewn up their bloody gashes after fights. I have watched them struggling to hold down their jobs in executive positions. I have watched them grow nervous and irritable under the strain of factory noise. I have monitored their hypertension. I have seen men working seven days a week to earn enough money to keep up their hire-purchase payments. I have seen men supporting two families, paying alimony to one and housekeeping money to the other. I have watched the conscientious bank manager develop his ulcer. I have known men who drank too much and smoked too heavily in order to maintain their composure under strain. I have seen man after man break his health, die prematurely of heart disease, succumb to cancer of the lung, commit suicide in old age, just because they have spent a lifetime trying to maintain an image of themselves as 'he-men'. I have wondered many times what there was that was so good about the male way of life, if it had to be lived in that way.

Of course, I have also seen women struggling under their 'feminine' roles. I have seen them driven into anxiety states over their lost external beauty, their ageing figures. I have watched them torn apart by jealousy. I have known women to be paralysed with fear when their marriages have broken up and they have not known how to manage on their own, because they had never had to do so before. I have watched women's tensions rise until they screamed at their children. I have seen their anxiety for their tired-out old men. I have lived with their sufferings, and have helped widows to learn in a slow and painful way to live again. I have wondered what was so fine about that way of life.

However, I have found far more women who found their joy in living. I have seen ambition reduced to a longing for the first smile from a newborn baby. I have seen women's gentleness with a child in pain. I have seen women turn their backs on advancement in order to be closer to their children. I have seen women pack their bags and uproot themselves for the sake of their husbands. I have watched women cradling their dying husbands in their arms. I have known the strong, enduring friendship of women. I have benefited from their generosity. I have cried with them and for them in their struggles to survive, to become whole people. I have known that there was something precious about the female way of life, something worthwhile which many men badly need to learn about.

When people think about partnership between women and men they have to ask themselves what they mean by the parity of partnership. There seems to be little point in women asking for parity, if all that will mean is that they will embrace a way of life which substitutes aggressive competition for friendship, and material success for the richness of life itself. At present, women who want to get to the top of

G

their professions have to adopt male life styles. The male life style seems, too often, to be a vertical style, in which one goal is set and attained, then another, and so on, until the top of the ladder is reached. The climber has to be dedicated and single-minded. He is able to pay little attention to other people, and he ignores interesting horizontal bypaths because to be interested in either people or diversions would be to reduce his efficiency in climbing to the top of the ladder.

Women who do not adopt this male life style enjoy a more horizontal way of living. They are able to wander off the rungs of the ladder to explore interesting byways. They may miss an important step in the vertical climb and so miss promotion. It is not that women eschew success, for they do not, but their idea of success is usually that of a full, varied life, in which status is not so important as achievement. Status, when it does come, is a pleasant by-product of achievement.

I believe that society has misunderstood the value of life to such an extent that vertical rise is rewarded by high pay and status, while horizontal achievement is ignored. It is my contention that horizontal exploration is as valuable as the vertical rise, and that both dimensions are needed if society is to be whole. Both kinds of activity should be able to find expression at all levels of society, and both should be recognised and rewarded alike. I think that parity between women and men means that women are needed in political, industrial and social life to provide the horizontal dimension. They do not have to do the same jobs as men in exactly the same way as men, but they should be able to bring their own abilities to bear on the same subject at equal status, and for equal reward. In economic terms, this policy might sometimes mean employing two people to carry out one task. In posts where a lot of creative thinking to the task in hand was essential, the extra money would be well spent. Madame Giradin, mayor of Geneva, has stated much the same view in this way :

I am violently opposed to any action that tends to differentiate between men and women, and am in favour of any effort and collaboration to deal with problems together. . . . I cannot see that any possible action can be specifically feminine. But women do have different attitudes. Women's interests are known to be differently constituted. The intuition, sense of reality, the ability to think in concrete terms and to see the practical consequences of an action, which are peculiar to women, are extremely useful in politics.[2]

I recognise that it is impossible to generalise. There are women who are gifted with such single-mindedness that they can pursue their goal vertically, and there are men who live their lives without thought of advancement. It may be that the ways in which women and men differ from each other at present, with regard to horizontal and vertical life styles, are largely the results of social conditioning. My point is that, at this particular point in history, women and men epitomise respectively the horizontal and vertical dimensions of living which are both necessary to society, and should both be recognised as of equal value.

Horizontal living is being adopted by an increasing number of men. It is true that men seldom feel entirely guiltless when they begin to live horizontally, but fortunately, more men are now able to live less frenetic lives, without feeling themselves to be less male because of their choice. Horizontal life styles are being recognised and allowed for in some places in the world. in 1973, for example, the Swedish Prime Minister, Olaf Pälme said :

> The men must also be emancipated. The new role of the man implies that he must reduce his contributions in working life – and maybe also in politics – during the period when he has small children. . . . Nobody should be forced into a pre-determined role on account of sex, but he should be given better possibilities to develop his or her personal talents.[3]

When men begin to value achievement instead of status they lose some of their fear of falling off the ladder of success. This enables women to accept their own life styles as good. They begin to see that they have some qualities which are valuable assets to the whole of society. This makes them more willing to take those assets into society instead of hiding them at home. It also helps women not to be so seduced by the male way of life that they twist themselves into conforming to the male pattern of doing things.

When women and men can look at each other and see what is good in the other sex, they are then in a position to learn to be themselves without fear of each other. Individuals find that they can live human and personal lives instead of living lives which are restricted through role conditioning. At that stage, when they have seen their own potentials and have recognised the potentials of other people, they are ready to learn how to combine vertical living with horizontal living in such a way that they become more fully human. They are free to become whole people. They are free to uncover the wholeness of the community.

8   The discovery of wholeness

*'They are ill discoverers that think there is no land,
when they can see nothing but sea.'*
(Francis Bacon)

The journey from slavery to freedom is not accomplished in a day.
Some people may never start out at all, either because they think that
there is no freedom, or because they think that the journey is too
hazardous. Those who do undertake the journey are the people who
have some idea that freedom is worthwhile. Once they have started, it
is all too easy for them to feel that they are floundering in a sea that is
endless. They may lose hope and come to doubt the existence of their
goal. They are more likely to feel that they themselves will never get
to the end of the journey. They know very well that many people have
already died on the way, and that many more will, before the journey
is done. Yet in people who are willing to make the journey, there is a
deep urge which drives them on. They are inspired by a vision of what
freedom might mean to them as individuals and to the community in
which they live. That vision has to do with perfection, with wholeness,
with the absolute.

   When I try to envisage wholeness or absolute perfection I know that
I am writing about what I do not yet know, but have only begun to see
in the distance : yet it is the vision of what might become possible
which inspires me, and so many other people, to go on trying to achieve
wholeness. Perhaps those who know themselves to be voyagers are expressing in their own way a mystery which is the heritage of all people.
However it is undertaken, the journey from slavery to freedom is essen-
tially a religious voyage, which demands faith. While I realise that
faith is a religious quality which is part of every human being, and is
expressed in many different ways, I myself undertook this particular
journey from the slavery of sexism to the freedom of wholeness because
of my Christian faith. It seems to me that the Gospel is all about a

voyage from slavery to freedom, the sort of freedom which makes people whole. Because I am a Christian, it is natural that my ideas about wholeness should have derived from a consideration about the person of Christ, who seems to me to have been the most whole person who ever lived. I believe that his wholeness is of importance to non-Christians as well as to those, like myself, who are Christians.

I know that I can only see the historical Christ through the eyes of writers who described him as they and others understood him, and who were writing with specific intentions and for selected audiences. I also know that I read the Bible with human eyes, and that it speaks to me in the light of my needs. It is therefore inevitable that I should make particular interpretations of the material we have about the life and teachings of Jesus. In thinking about the wholeness of Christ, I have not dissected each statement and each action of the man who lived 2000 years ago. I have taken an overall view of the man, his life and his relations with other people, and have allowed that view to enlarge my horizons, and to influence my vision of what Christ is doing in the world today.

The whole humanity of Christ enables us to become whole. He transformed humanity by assuming it. Julian of Norwich describes his work like this :

And our filthy dying flesh which the son of God took upon himself, like Adam's old coat, tight, threadbare, and too short, the Saviour transformed into something beautiful, fresh, bright and splendid, eternally spotless, full and flowing, fairer and richer, than even the clothing I had seen on the Father.[1]

In assuming human flesh Christ accepted his mother's flesh as his own. Within his one person Jesus incorporates all the elements of humanity. The union of these elements of humanity is so perfect in Christ that it is impossible to distinguish in him elements which can be labelled 'feminine' or 'masculine' : his life does not lend itself to that kind of analysis at all.

It is, I think, important to understand that Christ is the pattern for wholeness for women and men alike. If I identify the vertical life style as male and the horizontal life style as female I have to recognise that neither of these provides an analogy for a whole human life. It is the coming together of the two life styles which provides the model for a whole human life. Throughout his life on earth, Jesus looked upwards towards God, the Creator, and outwards towards those whom he had come to serve and lead to wholeness. This kind of symbolic analogy can transcend the partial truths about the differences between the vertical male and horizontal female life styles, so as to reveal that both are essential to wholeness, and that neither takes precedence over the other. If people try to hold this cruciform model of wholeness in mind as they read the Gospel narratives, they will discover for themselves that Christ shows women and men how to live their lives on a horizontal plane as well as a vertical one. St Paul seems to try to express this truth in his letter to the Ephesians :

> . . . that Christ may dwell in your hearts through faith; that you, being rooted and grounded in love, may have power to comprehend with all the saints what is the breadth and length and height and depth, and to know the love of Christ which surpasses knowledge, that you may be filled with all the fullness of God.[2]

When Christ came to his death his cross had a vertical upright and a horizontal cross-bar. Without both parts it would not have been a cross. The man who hung upon that cross united the vertical with the horizontal through the loving offering of his own body. His offering was made on behalf of the whole of humanity. Through his death, resurrection and ascension and through the work of the Holy Spirit, Christ becomes present to the world in the persons of his co-inheritors, women and men. As Dr John Robinson says in his book, *The Human Face of God* :

> The Christ now lives on – in the lives of those who represent now the human Face of God. The *prosopon*, the Face of the person of the Son, is henceforth the faces of men and women. The Son of Man is not replaced but represented by the shared life of the Spirit, which the Fourth Evangelist sees as the *alter ego* of Christ and appropriately names the Paraclete, the representative in court.[3]

Christ lives on in each woman and man. The cross is the symbol of what they are to become. It is the symbol of wholeness.

As a living human being Christ was a man. His sex was part of him : yet it was not his wholeness, and when he died he was freed from its limitations. Sexuality is an important and intimate part of every human being, yet it is not the whole of a person, nor can it be said that God relates only to femaleness or to maleness, or to a precise sexual balance in any one person. The image of God is to be found in heterosexual women and men, but it is also found in homosexuals, trans-sexuals, bisexuals, hermaphrodites and eunuchs. These people are not lacking in humanity because they are not the average. Christians have never found sexuality easy to understand, but to my knowledge, no theologian has ever said that anyone who is a homosexual, a bisexual or a trans-sexual by nature is automatically excluded from the 'in Christ' relation because of her or his sexual orientation. Their humanity is more important than their sex. In the same way, women as well as men are included in the 'in Christ' relation and always have been.

The human Christ was the representative of the whole of humanity, and yet, women and men who are alive now must still accept the limitations of their bodies. If they are to discover what whole living is, they will probably be able to catch the best glimpses of it in their joint relationships, for it is the paired relationship that represents the whole rather than women and men on their own. I want to look at this paired relationship in the context of the marital relationship, because I believe that women and men can discover their deepest solidarity with each other in the creative process of living together. In marriage they have the greatest chance of discovering a whole relationship, through which each partner can become a whole person. Although I have taken heterosexual marriage as a model of this intimate relationship. I believe that what I say also applies to any close relationship which enables two people to reveal their differences to each other without fear of the consequences of their openness to one another.

At the beginning of any union both partners will be aware of their differences and their different expectations of one another. In the course of living together the two partners discover that they change. Some parts of the self-centred needs of each are surrendered for the love of the other. Some parts of their separate personalities develop at the expense of other parts, because they are needed for the total good of the family. Each partner to a marriage remains a separate person, responsible for her or his own actions, but between them lies a corporate relation which is drawn from both, yet is separate from both. In this 'between' state a wife and husband share in a real way a joint and corporate responsibility for each other's actions in their relation with the rest of humanity. It is not easy to describe this corporate relation between wife and husband. In some couples the bond between two separate individuals is forged so strongly that it is as if there were a person called 'Mrs Jack Smith' or 'Mr Joan Brown' who represented the family to the outside world. In other couples each partner acts as an individual in relation to the outside world, and reserves the corporate relation for the intimacies of married life. It is important that people should recognise this 'between' area which lies within any close relationship. It is in this area of life that human beings can lose themselves and also find themselves. The 'between' areas provide them with a space in which they can grow in maturity and become more whole in relationship. The writer, François Chirpaz describes how this kind of relationship can affect each of the parties to it :

> Personal relationship is that meeting face to face in which I am recognised as different, in which I can recognise another as different, but in which the difference does not cause fear but joy at a human being, wholly his experience and whole existence brings me to an experience other than my own . . . anyone who has known what it is to discover the world which he thought he knew, by and through the perspective of another's experience, cannot be measured in qualitative or competitive terms. He knows that to give one's experience to others is no impoverishment, but opens it out on what of itself it would never have known.[4]

If people are to become more fully human through the discovery of each other in a whole relationship, they will have to become much more aware of these 'between' areas of life.

As a Christian, I believe that the 'between' areas, the interfaces of personalities and people, are areas where the Holy Spirit reveals persons to themselves and to each other. This activity of the Holy Spirit has been described by Bishop John Taylor in *The Go-Between God* in a way which I find easy to understand. He says :

> As a believer in the Creator Spirit I would say that deep within the fabric of the universe, therefore, the Spirit is present as the 'Go-Between' who confronts each isolated spontaneous particle with the beckoning reality of a larger whole and so compels it to relate to others in a particular way; and that it is he who at every stage lures the inert organisms forward by giving an inner awareness and recognition of the unattained.[5]

Bishop Taylor thinks that the activity of the Spirit may be recognised by three characteristics. He says that the Spirit enhances awareness, confronts people with the necessity of choosing, and encourages sacrifice :

> The Creator Spirit works from the inside of processes not only by startling his creatures into awareness and recognition and luring them towards ever higher degrees of consciousness and personhood, but also by creating the necessity for choice in one situation after another. And that choice arises always from the contrast between the actual and the potential, between things as they are and things as they might be . . . to embark upon a change of milieu, a change of habit, always feels like 'a little death'. Every step forwards into a fuller dimension of life is a kind of dying.[6]

Within each person there are many areas of 'between' that are the field for the activity of the Holy Spirit. Within each marriage, and between persons in relationship, there are areas where the Holy Spirit is at work leading partners on to wholeness, enabling the potential to become actual in them.

I know that potential has not yet become actual in most individuals or in most communities. Yet it is the potential which gives me hope for the future. It is the vision of the whole which inspires me, and many other people, to try to work out in very concrete terms a way of living together which will enable women and men to make their potentials realisable. It seems to me that if women and men want to discover what wholeness means, they have to get together on equal terms to think about their goals. It may be that they will have to re-think these goals in the light of their past mistakes, their joint dissatisfactions with life as they know it, and in the light of their joint needs for the future. What seems to me to be important is that women and men should re-think these goals together and never in isolation from each other. It is this conviction that prompts some people to insist that there must be equal representation of women and men in all processes where communal decisions have to be taken for the good of the whole community. This applies as much to the family as to social institutions like the Church and State. If people are to come together in this way they would have to leave behind them many of their cherished pre-conceptions about each other. They would have to die to their ideas that mothers can bring up children on their own. They would have to forget that men once thought it right to rule the world on behalf of women.

They might have to forgo the pleasure of single-sex institutions. They would certainly have to relinquish the habit of thinking about Father God and Mother Church. Women and men alike would have to surrender their prejudiced views about superiority and inferiority. Some people would undoubtedly lose the pleasure of being among those who always command : others would lose the equal pleasure of being among those who have no responsibility other than that of obedience. In dying to these very real satisfactions, people would, I believe, find their true selves. They would discover the joys of partnership with each other, the relief of being able to share decisions, the meaning of real community, the purpose of whole living for their own and the common good.

I do not minimise the difficulties which still lie ahead of women and men who seek to find their freedom in order to find their unity with each other, and their wholeness in each other. I, and they, face an uphill task, and yet I find myself echoing some words of Rilke :

> The demands which the difficult work of love make upon our development are more than life size, and as beginners we are not up to them, but nevertheless we must hold out and take this love upon us as burden and apprenticeship.[7]

As one apprentice among many others, I know the magnitude of the task ahead. I approach that task with realism. I am upheld by the courage of others, even when my own courage fails. I am sustained by other people's visions as well as my own. I know that if I do not myself reach journey's end, I must travel onwards for the sake of those who come after.

At the present time, I believe that there is an urgent necessity for women and men to make fresh beginnings in relationships by gathering together to reflect upon their common humanity, and to put into concrete action their joint discoveries about relationship. Reflection which is rooted in mutual experience can, I believe, enable women and men to go forward into the future with confident hope. I would not want to confine such encounter groups to people with religious awareness, but I do not think that people who are without religious affiliation can ignore the insights of people with such awareness. I certainly do not think that religious people can sit on the sidelines of life, or isolate themselves from the liberation struggles that are going on all around them. That is why I think that the Christian Church, and other religions, are urgently called to take up the task of contributing to the dialogue

between women and men which is going on in the world now. I think
that religious people will have to use new tools of theological reflection
for their task and that those tools will have to be forged by women
and men together. The old tools may have been useful in the past, but
they are no longer adequate for a task which must take into account
the scientific knowledge about sexuality and human nature that is available, and that must also take place in a world where communication
is vital to mutual understanding. Both the secular understanding of
religious language about sexuality and humanity, and the religious
understanding of secular language about liberation and the fullness of
life have so far been inadequate for people who want to get together
to discover what it means to be human. If 'religious' and 'non-religious'
people could together work out a common language, they might be able
to reach a fuller understanding of their sexuality and their humanity.

I am conscious that this particular book has been written from a
female and Christian perspective. It necessarily lacks a male and secular perspective. The book marks a stage in the search for wholeness.
It is my hope that it will open the way for fuller dialogue between
women and men of all beliefs, so that the next work on this subject
will be the result of their joint reflections. In coming together for that
kind of task people will be able to discover each other in a way that
should be liberating to all.

I do not know what the future for women and men will be. We must,
first of all, create the conditions which will enable us to discover more
fully what we may be capable of becoming. If we are to create these
conditions we need certain ingredients :

> Faith which can move mountains,
> Hope which will transform despair,
> Love which does not shrink from pain.

I believe that these ingredients are already present in all people through
the Holy Spirit, the strengthener, through Christ, the liberator, through
God, the source of all being. If we claim our inheritance we shall
become whole.

References and notes

Chapter 1

1. Group from 'Women in Media'. Both quotations used here are from their material.
2. Figures compiled from Newsletters of 'Women in Media', 'Women's Report', and the 'Fawcett Society Newsletter', 1973–74.
3. *Agenor*, 'Sexism in Europe', May–June, 1973.
4. 'Danger! Women at Work.' Report of N.C.C.L. Conference, 16.2.74. Ed. P. Hewitt. pp. 5–8.
5. House of Lords Select Committee, 'Special Report (2)', 18.4.73, p. 17.
6. 'Fawcett Society Newsletter', 14.10.74.
7. Private communication.
8. Commission of European Communities, 'Employment of women and the problems it raises for the member states of the E.E.C.', No. 8334.
9. Facts drawn from the resource material supplied by W.C.C. at 'Consultation on Sexism'.
10. Christa Lewek, 'Role of women in German Democratic Republic'. Paper given at Berlin consultation, 1974.
11. 'Danger! Women at Work', pp. 9–10.
12. Child Minder's Action Group information, 1974.
13. 'Danger! Women at Work', pp. 16–20.
14. *Agenor* report, May–June, 1973, and compiled British statistics.
15. Background information to Ms M. Colquhoun's 'Balance of Sexes Bill', 1974.
16. 'Fawcett Society Newsletter', 14.10.74.
17. Statistics from *Church of England Year Book*, 1973.
18. W.C.C. Information, Berlin, 1974.

Chapter 2

1. Clara Thompson, 'Some effects of the derogatory attitude towards female sexuality', *Psychiatry*, Vol. 13, 1950, pp. 349–54. Quoted in *Psychoanalysis and Women*. Ed. J. B. Miller. Pelican. 1974, p. 58.
2. S. Freud, 'Femininity', New Introductory Lectures, 1933. *Collected Works*, Vol. XXII, p. 116.
3. A. Adler, 'Sex', *Understanding Human Nature*, 1927. Quoted in *Psychoanalysis and Women*, p. 49.

4. C. Jung, *Collected Works*. Trans. R. F. C. Hall. Routledge and Kegan Paul, Vol. XV, p. 54.
5. A. Maslow, *The Farther Reaches of Human Nature*, Pelican, 1967, p. 167.
6. W. S. Churchill, *Onwards to Victory*. War Speeches. Ed. Chas Easy. Cassell, 1952, pp. 316–18.

Chapter 3

1. F. Dostoievski, *The Brothers Karamazov*, Part II, Bk v, Chap. 4.
2. A. Pope, 'An Essay on Man', Ep. ii, line 1.
3. S. Eimerl and I. De Vore, *The Primates*, Life Nature Library, Time-Life, 1966, pp. 165 ff.
4. P. Farb, *The Insects*, Life Nature Library, Time-Life, 1964, pp. 161 ff.
5. P. Tillich. Quoted in R. Dubos' *So Human an Animal*, Abacus, 1973, p. 102.
6. R. Dubos, *So Human an Animal*, p. 37.
7. *The Secret Sayings of Jesus according to the Gospel of Thomas*, Fontana, 1960, p. 185.

Chapter 4

1. The physical differences between women and men are well summarised in *Women and Work: Sex Differences and Society*. J. S. King. H.M.S.O., 1974.
2. *Ibid.*, p. 17.
3. D. C. McLelland, 'Dialogue on Women'. Quoted in a pamphlet published 1970 by the Grail Community, Lakeland, Ohio.
4. François Chirpaz, 'Masculin et Feminine', *Lumière et Vie*, No. 106, Jan./ Feb. 1972.

Chapter 5

1. Betty Friedan, *The Feminine Mystique*, Penguin, 1965, p. 63.
2. *Ibid.*, p. 25.
3. Private communication.
4. 'Women in Media' material used at opening session of W.C.C., 'Consultation on Sexism'.
5. *Ibid.*
6. Simone de Beauvoir, *The Second Sex*, Penguin, 1972, p. 19.
7. Opening Sermon, W.C.C. 'Consultation', 1974.
8. Resource paper, *Ibid.*
9. Peggy Ann Way, *Women's Liberation and the Church*, Association Press, 1970, p. 90.

Chapter 6

1. Partnership group, W.C.C. 'Consultation on Sexism'. Joint definition, 1974.
2. Jurgen Moltmann, *Religion, Revolution and the Future*, C. Scribner, 1969. Quoted in *A Reader in Political Theology*. A. Klee. S.C.M. Press, 1974, p. 51.

3. Mary Daly, 'A Call for the castration of sexist religion' in *Sexist Religion and Women in the Church*. Ed. A. Hageman. Association Press, 1974, p. 127.
4. Daphne Nash, 'Women's Liberation and Christian Marriage', *New Blackfriars*, May 1972.
5. Camillo Torres, *Revolutionary Priest*. Ed. J. Gerassi. J. Cape, 1971.
6. Jurgen Moltman. Quoted in 'Religion, Revolution and the Future' in *Political Theology*. A. Klee. p. 51.
7. These are all quotations from resource material at W.C.C. or personal knowledge.
8. *Church Times* Report, 9.8.74.
9. Dr Philip Potter, Address to participants in 'Consultation on Sexism'.
10. Robin Morgan. Quoted in Mary Daly, *Beyond God the Father*, Beacon Press, 1974. Also used in the opening session of the Consultation.

Chapter 7

1. *The Feminist Papers*. Ed. A. S. Rossi. Bantam, 1974, p. 426.
2. 'Sexism in Europe', *Agenor*, May–June 1973, p. 22.
3. *Ibid.*, p. 15.

Chapter 8

1. Julian of Norwich, 'Revelations of Divine Love'. Trans. Wolters. Penguin, p. 55.
2. Ephesians 3:18. R.S.V.
3. Dr J. Robinson, *The Human Face of God*, S.C.M. Press, 1972, p. 213.
4. F. Chirpaz, 'Masculin et Feminine', *Lumière et Vie*, Jan./Feb. 1972.
5. J. V. Taylor, *The Go-Between God*, S.C.M. Press, 1972, p. 31.
6. *Ibid.*, p. 33.
7. Rilke, *Letters to a Young Poet*. Quoted in a pamphlet published 1970 by the Grail Community, Lakeland, Ohio.

Selected books for further reading

The position of women in society is changing all the time. Feminist society newsletters and periodicals are the best way of keeping up to date. The following periodicals are always interesting:

Women's Report. Bimonthly. 2 Sherriff Court, Sherriff Road, London NW6 2AT.

Women Speaking. Quarterly. The Wick, Roundwood Avenue, Brentwood, Essex.

Spare Rib. Monthly. c/o New English Library, Bernards Inn, Holborn, London W.C.1.

Feminist classics like *The Feminist Papers*, edited by Alice Rossi and published by Bantam Books Ltd, Simone de Beauvoir's *The Second Sex*, Betty Friedan's *The Feminine Mystique* and Germaine Greer's *The Female Eunuch* are always worth re-reading, and are now widely available in paperback. People who want to see the other side of the picture should turn to Arianna Stassinopoulis' *The Female Woman* and Ainsley Mears' *The New Woman*.

If readers are unfamiliar with the medical and psychological material about women and men, the best short factual account is Dr J. S. King's *Women and Work: Sex Differences in Society*, published 1974 by H.M.S.O., High Holborn, London W.C.1. *Psychoanalysis and Women*, edited by Jean Baker Miller, published by Penguin Books in 1974, makes fascinating reading.

Women are seldom referred to in books on Liberation theology and Political theology that are available in England. However, for background material, *Seeds of Liberation*, ed. Alistair Kee, S.C.M., has one essay in it by a woman, and *A Reader in Political Theology*, edited by the same man, gives good background information to the various theological ideas which undergird many of the Christian liberation movements. You would have to go to America and Geneva to find books by women about women, and Mary Daly's *Beyond God the Father*, published in 1974 by Beacon Press, is an important work, as is *Sexist Religion and Women in the Church*, edited by Alice L. Hageman for the Association Press. In Geneva the W.C.C. has published 'Gladly We Rebel', *Risk*, Vol. 7, No. 1, 1971, and 'Words to the Churches – Voices of the Sisters', *Risk*, Vol. 10, No. 2, 1974. Mary Daly's earlier work, *The Church and the Second Sex*, published by Geoffrey Chapman Ltd, is available in England, but dates from 1968. The *New Blackfriars* quite often publishes articles on women and women in the Church.

I have not referred separately to women in the ministry of the Church, since I see life in holistic terms, but those who are interested in this subject may find much to interest them in the W.C.C.'s *Women – What Is Ordination Coming To?*, edited by Brigalia Bam, published 1970, and Christian Howard's 'The Ordination of Women', available from the Church Information Office, Church House, Westminster, London. S.W.1.